WORLD ENOUGH AND TIME

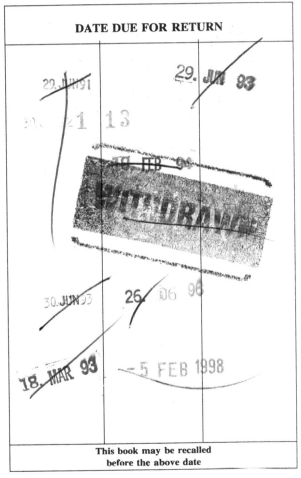

DATE DUE FOR RETURN

This book may be recalled
before the above date

A WORLD RESOURCES INSTITUTE BOOK

World Enough and Time
Successful Strategies for
Resource Management

ROBERT REPETTO

YALE UNIVERSITY PRESS
New Haven and London

Designed by James J. Johnson
and set in Melior Roman.
Printed in the United States of America by
Vail-Ballou Press, Binghamton, New York.

Library of Congress Cataloging-in-Publication Data

Repetto, Robert C.
    World enough and time.

    Includes index.
    1. Natural resources—Management.
2. Environmental policy.   3. Population policy.
4. Quality of life.
I. Title.
HC59.R43   1986   333.7   85–20180
ISBN 0–300–03648–5
ISBN 0–300–03649–3 (pbk.)

10   9   8   7   6   5   4   3   2   1

341702

Contents

Foreword

Few would deny that societies face challenges of unprecedented proportions as we approach the new century. Many of these challenges are worldwide in scope, binding together North and South, East and West in common concerns. This century's uniquely rapid expansion in technology, population, and economic activity has created the means for all to live more comfortably but has left the world deeply divided between an affluent minority and a growing population of poor. Growth and its by-products have also pressed more heavily on the natural cycles and systems on which all life depends, disrupting climate, displacing species and whole families of organisms from their place on earth, swamping the assimilative capacities of the environment—even as the knowledge and resources needed to create more sustainable patterns of living accumulate. Rapid innovation in information sciences, genetics, chemistry, military technology, and other fields is opening up new opportunities but is also creating risks different in kind and scale from those we have experienced until now.

Widely differing projections of the world's future have been advanced—some optimistic, some pessimistic. Ample grounds for both can be found in current experience. In the management of vital resources, in the buoyancy and dynamism of economic life, and in the welfare and stability of populations, some communities and countries have been remarkably successful. Others have fared dramatically less well. The possibilities in the next century diverge widely as success builds on success, or failure presses on failure.

This book grew from a conference the World Resources Institute sponsored in May, 1984, to explore the practical, tested steps that would lead to success in managing the world's resources and environmental and population pressures. Experts and experienced leaders from many countries and walks of life came together to identify the key challenges of the next twenty-five years and the best responses that experience has provided. This meeting, the Global Possible Conference, provided grounds for optimism, demonstrating that resources can be managed much more productively to provide widespread and lasting benefits and that tested and feasible actions can make the next century brighter for all.

Robert Repetto, the director of the Global Possible project, presents in this book the essential message and findings of the Global Possible Conference. He identifies key mechanisms—applicable across many resource sectors and issues, in developing and developed countries alike—that markedly improve the long-term performance of the approaches that are being used successfully today by governments, businesses, and citizens. *World Enough and Time* bespeaks possibility: grave as our resource, population, and environmental challenges are, they can be met with means that are within our reach and that further economic growth, sustained progress toward a poverty-free society, and other critical goals.

Much of the material for this book was drawn from the conference proceedings and from more technical and comprehensive papers commissioned from international experts on specific resource and population issues. These papers, together with cross-cutting essays providing the perspectives of history, economics, ecology, and ethics on the resource challenges of the future, are published in *The Global Possible: Resources, Development, and the New Century* (Yale University Press: 1985). Robert Repetto also edited this volume, which forms an interdisciplinary survey of international trends, issues, and policy directions. Longer and more technical, it will appeal to readers who want a more systematic and comprehensive presentation.

The World Resources Institute sponsored the Global Possible

Conference and both of these books as part of its continuing efforts to help governments, international organizations, the private sector, and others address a fundamental question: How can we meet basic human needs and nurture economic growth without undermining the natural resources and environmental integrity on which life, economic vitality, and international security depend? An independent policy research center created in 1982 with a grant from the John D. and Catherine T. MacArthur Foundation, World Resources works to provide accurate information and new perspectives on global resources and population, to identify emerging issues, and to develop politically and economically sound proposals.

JAMES GUSTAVE SPETH
President, World Resources Institute

Introduction

This book springs from an international conference organized by the World Resources Institute (WRI) in May 1984. The purpose of the conference was to identify significant and practical policy initiatives that would preserve natural resources and a healthy environment, while promoting a better quality of life for all and a marked improvement in the living standards of the world's disadvantaged. It tried to meet the need for a constructive policy perspective that neither assumes that challenges to future well-being from resource depletion, environmental degradation, population growth, and economic stress will simply resolve themselves without corrective action, nor arouses unwarranted fears that these challenges are unmanageable and must result in traumatic changes in social and economic life.

Because it underlined what can be done, at modest cost, to bring about dramatic improvements in the availability and use of water, energy, land, and other resources and to improve significantly the quality of human life, it was called the Global Possible Conference. To ensure that this optimistic view of the future was not utopian or speculative, the Global Possible project focused on proven technologies, tested innovations, and successful policy experiences. It sought out the feasible initiatives in each resource sector that, if widely adopted, would have the greatest beneficial effect on human welfare, the quality of the environment, and the state of the resource base as the world enters the next century.

In order to address these issues, the WRI enlisted the participation and capable assistance of a wide range of people: an able steering committee; a group of experts in specific resource areas and disciplines to provide background papers highlighting key challenges, successful models, and priority initiatives; additional expert panels to reconsider possible policy recommendations; seventy-five invited participants who, led by a very able conference chairman, spent three days contributing their rich and diverse experience in science, industry, government, and community affairs to the conference; and the wide-ranging talents of the Institute staff.

The insights that evolved from the background papers and from the extensive discussions before and at the conference provide ample confirmation of the possibilities available. Repeatedly, it emerged that options that would conserve resources were not only feasible but would also cost less and result in higher productivity than current practices. Many policy changes were identified that would improve the opportunities available to the world's disadvantaged and would significantly raise overall economic productivity as well.

Further, the promising opportunities for public and private sectors' initiatives are not unconnected in their effects, but strongly complementary. Action on one front promotes progress and strengthens initiatives on other fronts. Concerted efforts to bring to bear powerful mechanisms on key resource, population, and environmental challenges would have a magnified impact. Prompt actions, which can be taken now without great cost or disruption, will have an enormous effect over time, as the world passes into the next century.

This book is an effort to present the insights of the Global Possible project to a wider audience. It complements an edited volume of the technical background papers and a brief post-conference statement summarizing the principal findings.[1] Chapter 1

1. Robert Repetto, ed., *The Global Possible: Resources, Development, and the New Century* (New Haven: Yale University Press, 1985), and *Global Possible: Statement and Action Agenda* (Washington, D.C.: World Resources Institute, 1984).

shows the difference between the world's progress, as measured by modest upward (and sometimes declining) trends over time, and the possibilities, which are evident in the wide range of success and failure that countries and communities have experienced in meeting these challenges. It argues that the difference between sustained success and failure lies overwhelmingly in the policy realm. Chapter 2 attempts to give meaning to the term *sustainable development* by portraying the possibilities for world population, economic welfare, the state of the resource base, and the quality of the environment in the next century, should appropriate and prompt policy adjustments be adopted.

Chapter 3 highlights powerful mechanisms that are applicable to a wide range of resource issues and illustrates the success with which they have been applied. These mechanisms include (a) redirecting public policy and development efforts to address neglected problems of disadvantaged groups in society; (b) instituting reasonable limits on the use of community and common-property resources; (c) treating scarce resources as if they were scarce, not as if they were free, by pricing them at the cost of increasing their supply; (d) designing production systems as circular flows rather than linear processes; and (e) building management capability for environmental protection and efficient resource use. Although these are not the only important policy instruments, these alone would ensure sustainable resource use if pursued with strong political and public support.

Chapter 4 summarizes the policy analyses undertaken for nine major resource sectors. The sectoral diagnoses and prescriptions draw heavily on working group reports drafted for the conference, reviewed by expert panels, and intensively scrutinized and revised by the conference participants. They present in a highly condensed form the key issues in each sector, important objectives for public policy, and a set of high-payoff, reasonable-cost initiatives that can be undertaken by governments, international agencies, science, industry, and private voluntary agencies. Chapter 5 pursues the implementation of these initiatives further by exploring the special roles each of these institutional groups can play.

It should be obvious that this book owes much to the many participants in the Global Possible project: the steering committee, authors, expert panels, participants, and colleagues at the World Resources Institute. But special acknowledgment is due to the contributions of Gus Speth, Jessica Mathews, and Kathleen Courrier of WRI, who supplied most of the inspiration and much of the perspiration that went into the project.

CHAPTER ONE

Progress and Possibility

Critics and actors on the world's stage have contended throughout the past decade whether a tragedy is being played out or a comedy. Some intellectuals foresee an ending in which all live happily ever after, others a catastrophe with corpses strewn across the proscenium. Both schools find ample evidence in the events of the present to support their predictions. The debate has left the academy and entered the forum. Optimism has served as a political platform, pessimism as a political epithet. However, nations, communities, and individuals are not merely players in this drama, but also playwrights, and the script for the next century is being written today, just as today's scenes were plotted years ago.

During the twenty-two years from 1960 to 1982, world per capita income grew at an average rate of 3.5 percent per year, slightly more than doubling its original level. Yet consider two countries: Korea, a middle-income country with a per capita income in 1982 of $1,910, and Ghana, a low-income country with a per capita income of $360, less than one-fifth as high. Population density is eight times greater in Korea than in Ghana—the Gold Coast—which by any standard is more generously endowed with natural resources. During these twenty-two years, income in Korea rose on average by 6.6 percent per year, doubling and redoubling. In Ghana, income actually fell at an average compound rate

1

of 1.3 percent over this entire period, leaving Ghanaians only three-fourths as well off in 1982 as they were in 1960. In 1960, Korea and Ghana had exactly the same per capita income.

The same enormous range of performance is evident in many other demographic, environmental, and economic trends. On average, for all low- and middle-income countries, per capita food production rose by a modest 10 percent between 1960 and 1982, whereas cereal imports rose 50 percent. But Asia made considerable progress while Africa fell backward. In Sri Lanka, where sixteen million people inhabit an area the size of Ireland, per capita food production increased 54 percent and cereal imports were halved. In Egypt, per capita production fell 15 percent and imports nearly doubled.

The population growth rate in the developing countries, excluding China, remained approximately constant at 2.5 percent per year over these decades. But this aggregate masks enormous variation. The rate of natural increase in Cuba fell from 2.5 percent in 1960 to 1 percent in 1982, the fertility rate fell to replacement level, and life expectancy reached seventy-five years, the same level as in the United States. In South Africa, a country whose per capita income is nearly twice as great, the rate of natural increase rose during these years from 2.4 to 3.1 percent, life expectancy is sixty-three years (the average rate of China and India), and the fertility rate remains twice the replacement level.

Among all low-income countries, on average, the percentage of girls aged six to eleven enrolled in primary school rose from 34 to 81 percent between 1960 and 1982 (from 25 to 58 percent if China and India are excluded). In Kenya, the increase was from 30 to 100 percent, whereas in Pakistan, a country with the same per capita income, the improvement was only from 13 to 31 percent.

There are similarly wide differences in rates of resource depletion. A recent Food and Agriculture Organization (FAO) study of clearing and degradation of tropical forests concluded that the overall rate of clearing of closed tropical forests in the 1980s is about 0.6 percent per year, but there is wide variation from country to country. In the central African region, including the Congo, Zaire, and Cameroon, the rate is as low as 0.2 percent annually, whereas in the West African coastal nations of Ivory Coast and Nigeria, the rate may be as high as 4 to 6 percent. In Latin America, the rates range from 0.4 percent in Brazil, where despite widespread clearing enormous reserves remain, to more than 3.5 percent per year in Costa Rica, El Salvador, and Paraguay, where large-scale commercial ranching has taken over previously forested areas.[1]

Countries differed tremendously in their response to changing scarcities and costs of energy resources. In the member countries of the Organization for Economic Cooperation and Development (OECD), total energy demand fell on average by 0.3 percent per year, whereas gross domestic product (GDP) increased by 2.1 percent per year. Among the middle-income developing countries, in which commercial energy sources are more important than noncommercial sources, energy consumption slowed from an annual rate of increase of 8 percent between 1960 and the first oil crisis in 1974, to a rate of 5.4 percent from 1974 to 1981. Growth in GDP slowed marginally, from 6 to 5.4 percent between the 1960s and 1970s, implying gains in energy efficiency. In the Dominican Republic, however, production growth accelerated from 4.5 to 6 percent between the two decades, even though half of all export earnings had to be spent on energy imports. But energy consumption, which had been rising by 14 percent per year up to the oil crisis, fell subsequently by 1.2 percent annually until 1981. Energy efficiency increased significantly. Similarly, in Singapore, production growth barely flickered, declining form 8.8 percent annually in the 1960s to 8.5 percent in the 1970s, but the growth of energy consumption fell from 9.4 percent before the oil crisis to 1.6 percent thereafter. Despite having no energy resources whatever, Singapore ended the period with a debt service burden of less than 1 percent of annual exports. By contrast, Mexico, an oil exporter, experienced a decline in GDP growth rates between decades from 7.6 to 6.4 percent, despite the oil boom, and saw annual growth in energy consumption accelerate from 7.4 to 9.3 percent after 1974. Mexico ended the period in economic crisis, with debt service obligations 30 percent of export earnings.

1. J. P. Lanly, *Tropical Forest Resources*, FAO Forestry Paper no. 30 (Rome: FAO, 1983).

These wide variations in performance are one reason for the wide range of uncertainty in forecasts. Optimistic or pessimistic assumptions extrapolated into the future must lead to very divergent predictions when the differences in performance are so great. Deforestation at 2 percent per year would result in the loss of three-fourths of present forest acreage by the year 2050. At the rate of 0.2 percent, only one-eighth would disappear. Population projections based on the assumed continuation of past trends imply that the world's population will ultimately stabilize at about 14.5 billion. If projections are based on diffusion of the most rapid declines in fertility observed anywhere, the ultimate world population size is projected to be just half that. Continued increases in fossil energy conversion at the rates of this decade would surely result in large shifts in climate, precipitation patterns, and shorelines by the middle of the next century. Projections of energy use based on rapid diffusion of energy-efficient technologies show that these momentous changes can be avoided.

There are ample grounds in experience for both optimistic and pessimistic assumptions. The contrasts described above could be matched in any other realm of performance. The gap between best performance and failure is enormous. What is important is that these wide variations in performance are attributable not to chance events or to uneven resource endowments, but to identifiable differences in policy orientations and actions. Korea's economic success and Ghana's struggles are due to the economic policies they have followed. Cuba's demographic transformation and South Africa's lagging transition are due mainly to differences in their social policies. The improvements that Singapore and the Dominican Republic made in energy efficiency stemmed from their energy policies and adaptation to external economic changes. Therefore, disputes between optimistic and pessimistic forecasters are implicitly disputes about the future of policy changes.

The critical issues arise not so much from the modest changes in the average indicators of progress but from this wide variation in experience. That many trends, overall, have been modestly upward is of limited interest and relevance. The example of successful experiences demonstrates how much better the record could be if the policies and actions underlying those successes were followed more widely. The unsuccessful experiences are reminders of the possible consequences if wrong choices are pursued.

Although food production per capita rose by 10 percent in low-income countries taken together over the past two decades, it fell significantly in fifteen out of thirty-four. The rate of growth of total population in the developing countries declined between the 1970s and 1980s, but it accelerated in almost half of the individual countries. Of sixty-four developing countries for which estimates are available, one-third managed to raise the level of GDP per unit of commercial energy consumed, an aggregate measure of energy productivity, during the decade of the 1970s. Two-thirds did not. Since the record is so mixed, the important question is not the level of the average performance but how to tip the balance toward more widespread success.

This tension between success and failure continues to heighten as human power over the planet grows and becomes increasingly concentrated in the leadership of few organizations. World war, an invention of this century, now threatens the extinction of human life in a nuclear exchange of hours or minutes. World markets for energy, food grains, and credit, supply an increasing share of world demands and are subject to disruptions that originate in national decisions that have worldwide repercussions. The environmental impacts of economic activity are no longer only local in scale but are capable of altering the planet's climate and primary productivity. Already one-half of the biosphere's net primary productivity is diverted to human uses. As economic and population expansion continues, the realm in which self-regulating natural systems can regenerate themselves unperturbed by human activities shrinks. The margin for error in decisions that can inflict irreversible change on the resource base is diminishing.

Those decisions need not be voyages into uncharted waters. In most directions, innovators have already gone ahead. Rapid progress consists in following quickly to catch up with the leaders. At the time of the Europeans' arrival, the potato had not yet reached Mexico from Peru, nor had the tea bush reached India from China. Now, the enormous gains in transportation and information technologies that have been made can broadcast innovations around the world almost instantaneously. Successful experiences are accessible to emulators to an unprecedented degree.

Yet the possibilities still far exceed the actual. The gap between the average and the leading edge is wide. In agriculture in developing countries, the yield reserve estimated by the FAO, based on the gap between average reserves and those obtainable from known technologies applicable to the areas considered, ranges from 300 to 400 percent for various major crops. The gap between actual and biologically potential yields established by research stations is much larger, from 500 to 1,000 percent for rice in the tropics, for example.

The potential improvement in the efficiency of energy use, just through adoption of known technologies, is enormous. Fuel use for space heating can be reduced in the United States by one-half or two-thirds in existing houses and by three-quarters in new houses through investments in insulation, storm windows, caulking, and weatherstripping. Similarly, the most efficient appliances on the market today use only one-half to one-third the energy of the average in use, and more efficient wood-burning stoves for the billion people dependent on fuelwood can triple the useful energy derived from burning wood.

In industry, large energy savings are possible in the major energy-intensive industries. In the U.S. chemical industry, energy efficiency rose 3.9 percent per year between 1972 and 1979 because of better "housekeeping," heat recovery, and process design. Steelmakers in the United States use 60 percent more energy per ton of steel than the Japanese do and twice as much as new Swedish technologies require. Technologies under development require only one-third as much energy per ton as is currently consumed in the U.S. steel industry.

The gap is obvious in the transportation sector. In the United States, the average mileage per gallon of gasoline in 1981 was sixteen, when the Volkswagen Rabbit achieved thirty-one mpg and the Volkswagen diesel forty-five. The 1984 Honda Civic CRX recorded fifty-two mpg in city-highway mileage tests run by the Environmental Protection Agency (EPA), and experiments suggest almost eighty mpg can be achieved with only modest advances over today's technology.

Equally impressive improvements are available in energy production. The World Bank, in conjunction with energy sector lending, has raised petroleum recovery threefold in Turkey's largest field by introducing carbon dioxide injection techniques previously used only in advanced oil-producing countries and has raised natural gas recovery tenfold through hydraulic fracturing.[2] These technologies are widely applicable elsewhere.

The examples can be multiplied almost indefinitely. While New Yorkers lean on their horns in daily traffic jams, Hong Kong drivers carry electronic sensors under their cars to record their entry into congested downtown areas and pay congestion fees based on their contribution to peak traffic loads. Indian farmers, who flood their fields with water delivered through unlined canals, lose 85 percent of the irrigation water potentially available for uptake by plant roots, but Israeli and California farmers using drip irrigation precisely scheduled to crop requirements use 85 percent of the water potentially available.

The possibility of widespread and rapid improvement in the efficiency and productivity of resource use is not utopian. It rests on successful experience and tested innovation. To a large extent, the models are already available for adaptation and diffusion. Since the pace of technological change is quickening, the application and management of what is known is an ever-growing challenge and opportunity. In particular, institutions must also adapt more rapidly to keep pace. Advances in information technology, biotechnology, energy technologies, and others push on institutions that evolved in an earlier and technologically simpler time. Property rights over computer programs, bioengineering techniques, and novel intellectual products must be assured, and standards that ensure compatibility of processes and products across international boundaries must be developed if the benefits of technological innovation are to be diffused rapidly.

Further, the direction of future innovation is under the influence of present policy. Innovation is determined by both scientific possibilities and potential economic rewards. When the price of fossil fuels rose dramatically, a flood of new products and pro-

2. World Bank, *The Energy Transition in Developing Countries* (Washington, D.C.: World Bank, 1983).

cesses for energy conservation and alternative energy supplies came onto the market. When cobalt prices rose in the mid-1970s as supplies from Zaire of this supposedly critical mineral were cut off, the search for new technologies and substitutes was spurred. Cobalt-free magnets were developed, and ceramics began to be used instead for turbine blades. New processes for reducing or treating hazardous wastes emerged when these wastes could no longer be cheaply discarded in the environment.

The stream of innovation constantly shifts its channel. The currents of progress quicken in countries that were backwaters, while past leaders stagnate. The European nations that forged the industrial revolution are no longer in the forefront, and Asian nations surge ahead. Although the life cycles of nations and the sources of cultural dynamism remain mysterious, finding and us-ing the policy levers that sustain dynamism in technological and institutional innovation and channeling that energy into socially desirable directions are of critical importance in the long run.

Persuasive arguments have been advanced that a fundamental policy challenge is to vitiate zero- and negative-sum games throughout society—situations in which people can benefit most by actions that impose equal or greater costs on others—and create positive-sum games—situations in which the best gains result from decisions that also benefit others. When the former predom-inate in a society, the sum effect of people's efforts to improve their lot may be stagnation or loss. When the latter prevail, overall welfare and productivity increase.[3]

Negative-sum games are distressingly common. The extreme example is lawlessness, which threatens the rights and property of some with arbitrary usurpation by others. Those threatened spend resources to protect their rights and property and forego opportunities that appear risky. At the international level, law-lessness and insecurity compel nations to expend enormous re-sources on military preparations.

Some see rapid population growth in poor countries as itself a negative-sum game. Parents without better alternatives hope to find willing family workers and a source of old age security in

3. Lester Thurow, *The Zero-Sum Society* (New York: Basic Books, 1980); Mancur Olson, *The Rise and Decline of Nations* (New Haven: Yale University Press, 1982).

large families. Their many children, however, grow up in a world where farms have been fragmented and subdivided, employment opportunities are scarce, and educational requirements are stiffer. Providing women better opportunities than perpetual motherhood, establishing effective health services to ensure children's survival, and creating opportunities for better educated youths alter this "game" and create incentives to have smaller families.

The common-property status of many natural resources creates a destructive negative-sum situation. Without regulation, firms can minimize the cost of disposing of manufacturing wastes by discharging them into surface impoundments or wells, often imposing much greater costs than their savings on households whose water supply is poisoned as a result. Legal provisions that effectively impose liability on firms for such damages or penalties for improper waste disposal that approximate the potential damages provide the incentives for firms to seek economical alternatives.

Workers in uncompetitive industries can protect their earnings by securing protection against imports, but usually at a much greater cost to consumers in the form of higher prices. In the United States, for example, each job saved through import controls in the steel and textile industries costs consumers an estimated $80,000 to $140,000 per year, and the additional cost is slower growth in more competitive industries. Where protection is pervasive, productivity and living standards stagnate. Policies that foster mobility through investments in retraining and compensation for adjustment costs and stimulate investment and expansion in growing industries reward workers and entrepreneurs who raise productivity.

Groups within society can protect their share of national income in an inflationary spiral, but only at the cost of shifting resources toward short-term speculative uses instead of long-term investments. People of means can shift the burden of taxes to others by taking advantage of tax shelters, but only at the cost of lower overall productivity as resources are diverted to investments that offer a lower real return before taxes. Fiscal policies that put tax codes on a simpler and fairer basis can redirect investors' attention toward socially profitable investments.

Fortunately, positive-sum situations also abound. The great advantage of market transactions is that all the participants, in their own estimation, are made better off by the voluntary exchange. By ensuring that the distribution of resources, power, and information is sufficiently equal that all do benefit by market exchanges, and by creating an institutional and legal framework that facilitates voluntary transactions, policy can encourage a better use of resources.

For example, industrial cogenerators of process steam and electricity typically save as much as 30 percent of the fuel energy needed to produce these services separately. In the United States, only 5 percent of industrial electricity is cogenerated, whereas European countries cogenerate four or five times as much. Rulings under the U.S. Public Utilities Regulatory Policies Act (PURPA) requiring utilities to interconnect physically with cogenerators and purchase or sell electricity at incremental cost, and clarifying the regulatory status of cogeneration facilities, opened the way to rapid expansion of this source of improved efficiency. Cogeneration is expected to double its share as an industrial energy source by the end of the century.

The benefits of such policy and institutional changes are large. In the western United States, water law has severely impeded improvements in water efficiency and conservation.[4] The beneficial use doctrine that entitles users to only that amount of water that they can put to good use has been interpreted to imply that one who transfers water to another, to whom its value is greater, is not able to put the water to beneficial use and can be stripped of rights to it. Similarly, the appurtenance doctrine, which holds that water rights are tied to particular pieces of land for which they were granted, has impeded users from conserving water in one irrigated field to use on another or to transfer to another user. The doctrine of "prior appropriation" has made difficult the transfer of any water to another use, no matter how valuable, if the transfer would affect water availability to another right-holder. States that have relaxed and rationalized such restrictions have been able to achieve greater efficiency through reallocation of water among

4. L. M. Hartman and Don Seastones, *Water Transfers: Economic Efficiency and Alternative Institutions* (Baltimore: Johns Hopkins Press for Resources for the Future, 1970).

users as demands for water change. A recent study in California demonstrated that a water transfer of four hundred thousand acre-feet per year between the Imperial Irrigation District and the Metropolitan Water District of Southern California would raise the productivity of the water by $100 to $250 per acre-foot and save $500 million in construction costs to bring in additional supplies.[5]

The opportunities for constructive policy change are large. If positive-sum games are encouraged, nations will enjoy more efficient use of resources and faster productivity growth; if negative-sum games predominate, nations will stagnate or decline. Over the long run, the difference in performance is enormous. Predictions about the future are really predictions about the policy orientations that will prevail.

5. Robert Stavins, *Trading Conservation Investments for Water* (Berkeley, Calif.: Environmental Defense Fund, 1983).

CHAPTER TWO

A Choice of Futures

Disturbing visions of the human condition early in the next century are not difficult to draw from the present situation. Population growth at the high end of the projected range, which corresponds to a continuation of current rates of *decline* of birth and death rates, would exacerbate already serious problems for many developing countries. The number of people in Bangladesh would have doubled, with another doubling ahead, in a country where already more than one-third of the rural population is landless, the average size of a farm-holding has declined from 3.5 acres in 1960 to 1.3 acres today, more than 40 percent of the rural poor survive on less than 80 percent of the FAO's minimum caloric intake requirement, and real wages in agriculture have fallen by 50 percent during the past twenty years.

Many more people could be exposed to the squalor of slums and deteriorating environmental conditions in Third World cities. Nairobi, where 40 percent of the inhabitants now occupy shacks in illegal shantytowns with no piped water, sewers or drains, lighting, or access roads, would grow from one million to more than five million people early in the next century. Uncontrolled air pollution could contribute to elevated levels of pneumonia, bronchitis, and lung cancer in the industrial cities in the Third World, where respiratory diseases already are the leading overall cause of death.

The loss of agricultural land through erosion, salinization, and waterlogging could undermine the livelihood of millions of cultivators and impede efforts to raise agricultural production. Thirty-five percent of the world's land area, including significant parts of the productive regions of the Northern Hemisphere, are at risk. In the Sudan, for example, where per capita food production declined 13 percent during the past decade, the deterioration of rangelands is moderate to severe. There, rain-fed croplands are increasingly afflicted by declining soil fertility and soil crusting due to unsuitable cropping practices, leading to lower yields and abandoned farms. Irrigated Sudanese lands are deteriorating severely because of poor management and siltation from upstream erosion. Deforestation is very severe, especially around the cities, contributing to further erosion and the encroachment of sand dunes from the Libyan desert.[1] These processes at work in the Sudan and other arid and semiarid regions, destroying the productivity of an estimated twenty million hectares per year, could become more severe as pressures on agricultural land intensify.

In the industrialized world, disturbing environmental trends persist. In the United States, there are more than fifteen thousand uncontrolled sites containing hazardous wastes in the EPA's emergency and remedial response inventory and more than eighty thousand sites in the nation with contaminated surface lagoons, pits, and ponds. Tests of underground drinking water supplies in 954 cities with populations exceeding ten thousand people found contamination by hazardous wastes leached from landfills and surface impoundments in 275. Despite this threat from waste disposal in the past, more than one metric ton per person of hazardous wastes is being generated and added to landfills and surface impoundments each year, and progress in siting safe disposal and treatment facilities over local community opposition is painfully slow.

From 1950 to 1980, worldwide emissions of carbon dioxide rose at an average rate of 4 percent per year. Energy models that forecast future increases in emissions of carbon dioxide and other

1. Leonard Berry, "Assessment of Desertification in the Sudano-Sahelian Region, 1977–84," Report to the United Nations Sudano-Sahelian Office (Clark University, Worcester, Mass., January 1984).

greenhouse gases at less than half those rates predict substantial climate changes: a mean rise in surface temperatures of 3°C, plus or minus 1.5°C, in the first half of the next century. The implications of such a shift in temperature are uncertain but substantial, since a range of 5°C covers the entire temperature variation of the past 125,000 years. The implications include major shifts in precipitation and runoff that could imperil agricultural production in important temperate farming regions, more frequent occurrences of damaging temperature extremes, and possible rises in sea level of two to twelve feet, which could cause major flooding and storm damage in coastal areas.

These scenarios are not forecasts, nor are they predictions. But they are possibilities, and they could result from policy choices or from failure to act. They are not implausible because, in part or in embryo, they already exist. Although there are many visions of a desirable future, none includes scenarios such as these.

In fact, there is considerable consensus on the basic elements of a more desirable future, resting in part on the physical facts of life. There is consensus that the human population must be stable, as it was for most of human existence. Rates of population growth even remotely approaching those experienced in this century are unsustainable over the next. However, the time it takes to reach stability, the size of the human population at stability, and the way in which stability is achieved are critical. A balance of births and deaths with life expectancies around the world at seventy-five years, the current level in the industrial countries, implies that crude birth rates must be less than ten per thousand—less than one-third the current level in the low-income countries.

There is further consensus that economic growth conceived and organized as an assembly line, drawing virgin materials into the production process at one end and spewing finished goods ultimately to be discarded along with waste materials out the other end, is unsustainable. The capacity of natural systems to withstand disruption, either by the intrusion of wastes or by the harvesting of part of the stock, is limited. Continuing expansion of these activities at anything like 4 percent per year, the rate of growth of the world economy, is impossible. The assimilative and rejuvenative capacities of natural systems would ultimately be overwhelmed, and the natural resource base on which we depend would be impoverished. Future economic growth must emulate natural productivity, recycling materials and energy to a much larger extent. There must be continual reduction in the generation of wastes and the use of virgin materials per unit of output and continual substitution of more abundant materials for those that become more scarce.

There is consensus that more attention must be paid to the future implications of current economic policies. A gigantic experiment with natural systems is now under way, and by the time the results are known with certainty, all the risks will have been undergone. Since climate change will continue for decades after the accumulation of greenhouse gases stops, policies must be adopted before the experiment is resolved if risks are to be avoided. Similarly, since population growth also will continue for decades after the world reaches replacement fertility, the consequences of a world of eleven or fourteen billion people cannot be known for sure when policies to avert it are pursued. The need for an anticipatory response to such risks is increasingly recognized.

This idea is summarized in the goal of sustainable development—a development strategy that manages all assets, natural resources, and human resources, as well as financial and physical assets, for increasing long-term wealth and well-being. Sustainable development, as a goal, rejects policies and practices that support current living standards by depleting the productive base, including natural resources, and that leave future generations with poorer prospects and greater risks than our own.

It is clear in the economic sphere what is not sustainable development. The support of current consumption through foreign borrowing that leaves the next generation with a heavy burden of debt service obligations is not. That is not a strategy that the next generation, and the next, could follow without impoverishment. The failure to maintain the quality and skills of the next generation by underinvestment in the quality and availability of education is not. Analogously, the support of current consumption levels by depletion and mining of soils, forests, fisheries, and energy resources, so that the future productivity of natural resources is impaired, is not.

The core of the idea of sustainability, then, is the concept that current decisions should not impair the prospects for maintaining or improving future living standards. This is strikingly similar to John Locke's criterion for judging appropriations of natural resources—that such property claims should be considered valid only if they leave "as much and as good for others." This implies that our economic systems should be managed so that we live off the dividend of our resources, maintaining and improving the asset base. Ironically, this principle bears much in common with the theoretical concept of income that practical accountants seek to measure: the greatest amount that can be consumed in the current period without reducing prospects for consumption in the future. Accountant and philosopher agree on the basis of sustainability.

This does not imply that sustainable development demands the preservation of the current stock of natural resources or any particular mix of human, physical, and natural assets. As development proceeds, the composition of the underlying asset base changes. In resource-rich countries such as the United States, abundant natural resources were exploited rapidly and early to finance the creation of ports, roads, houses, farms, and—later—factories. Other assets became much more important than natural resources. Land, which was the preponderant asset in colonial times, amounted to only one-third of total tangible assets by 1900 and accounts for only about one-fourth now. At the same time, human capital—the valuable skills and training embodied in the population and labor force—has risen to dominate our national wealth. Human capital, depending on the means used to estimate its value, now constitutes between 50 and 90 percent of all assets in the United States. The composition of U.S. national wealth has changed dramatically, but the increase in total assets per head has been impressive. During the entire period of 1900 to 1980, per capita total assets, conventionally defined (excluding human capital), rose by 1.7 percent per year, doubling and redoubling, and the rate of increase would be appreciably faster were the growth in human capital included, since that has doubled and redoubled on a per capita basis just since 1953.[2] This accumulation of national assets has supported a sharp rise in living standards.

2. R. W. Goldsmith, *The National Balance Sheet of the United States* (Chicago: University of Chicago Press for the National Bureau of Economic Research, 1982).

Although sustainable development is compatible with dramatic changes in the asset base, some changes are irreversible and can entail serious long-run losses. There are a limited number of good storage sites for impoundment of surface waters to be used for irrigation and hydroelectric power generation. Most have already been developed. When their capacity is diminished by siltation, the sites are, for practical purposes, irreversibly lost and no longer available to fulfill rising demands for agricultural products and renewable energy. Similarly, when species become extinct, their potential value in scientific research, in developing improved agricultural strains or new pharmaceutical products is irretrievably lost. The million species extinctions likely to occur during the rest of this century, if strong action is not taken, will extinguish options of inestimable value. Therefore, sustainable development implies that assets must be managed for the long run, taking into account their possible value in the future as well as their current value.

The three bases for sustainable development are scientific realities, consensus on ethical principles, and considerations of long-run self-interest. There is broad consensus that pursuing policies that imperil the welfare of future generations, who are unrepresented in any political or economic forum today, is unfair. Most would agree that an economic system and policies that consign a large share of the world's population to deprivation and poverty are also unfair. But pragmatic self-interest reinforces that belief. Poverty, which denies people the means to act in their own long-run interest, underlies the deterioration of resources and the growing population pressures in much of the world and affects everyone. Further, the threat of destruction from military confrontation in a world of increasing nuclear proliferation is so strong and imminent that there is urgent need to reduce conflict and its sources and to build mechanisms for cooperative, mutually beneficial approaches to world problems. Even if the chances of a nuclear outbreak in any year were only one in a hundred, the odds *against* our surviving the next century without a nuclear catastrophe would be three to one.

For the goal of sustainable development to be fulfilled, then, the Global Possible Conference declared that several critical transitions must be completed:

- A demographic transition to a stable world population of low birth and death rates
- An energy transition to high efficiency in production and use and increasing reliance on renewable sources
- A resource transition to reliance on nature's "income" without depletion of its "capital"
- An economic transition to sustainable development and a broader sharing of its benefits
- A political transition to a global bargain grounded in complementary interests between North and South, East and West.

The results of the many assessments that provided the foundation for the Global Possible Conference suggest that such a prosperous and sustainable future is attainable. Population can stabilize before it doubles again, with much improved health and life expectancies around the world. This will happen only if the poorer half of the world's population, who probably consume less than 10 percent of the world's output, can find productive jobs, access to land, credit, training, or other resources by which to raise their incomes; only if women throughout the world can find alternatives to early marriage and many children; and only if basic and inexpensive health and family planning services are available to all.

Agricultural production can expand to meet all future demands, including the needs of the undernourished, without exerting destructive pressures on marginal lands, water resources, or ecological systems. But this will happen only if farming systems and agricultural technologies that match land capabilities are developed and explained to the world's farmers; only if incentive systems that farmers respond to reflect accurately the true value of agricultural outputs and inputs and the true costs of resource use; and only if farmers and herders are not pushed onto marginal land by population growth and increasing land concentration.

Economic growth can be sustained with markedly lower energy inputs, and these can be supplied by a mix of sources that do not imperil the climate or the natural environment. The buildup of carbon dioxide in the atmosphere can be contained at concentrations that limit the risk of climatic disruption, and energy services can be provided without exacerbating nuclear insecurity, international economic instability, air and water pollution, and other energy-related problems. This will happen only if energy prices and energy policies are structured to achieve the enormous potential that exists for further energy conservation and improved efficiency in energy use and if energy plans and decisions are based on the full costs and risks of energy alternatives.

Further, forest resources, essential to the functioning of many ecological systems and as energy and income sources for much of the world's population, can be stabilized and expanded through better management and productive investment. The loss of biological diversity can be arrested, and the potential of this enormous resource better explored and used in agriculture, medicine, and industry. Nonfuel minerals and materials can be supplied over the long run at affordable prices through the efficient movement of capital, technology, and commodities in international markets. Environmental pollution can be markedly reduced and the quality of the environment preserved by more efficient resource recovery and source abatement. Cities, even in low-income countries experiencing rapid urbanization, can be made healthier and more livable if individual and community initiatives are encouraged and mobilized, and if public investments concentrate on providing basic urban services to all neighborhoods at standards of service all can afford to pay for.

These possibilities are not expensive to achieve. In fact, they are usually less costly than the present course, and many represent the least-cost approach to the problem. Basic health and family planning services that can cut mortality and morbidity rates by half and encourage much more effective protection against unwanted pregnancies can be provided in most Third World countries at an annual cost of $2 to $4 per capita, much of which can be recovered from clients. This is less than most Third World countries are now spending on health care and less than many public health services alone spend.

Safe drinking water through appropriately designed community systems can be supplied in low-income urban neighborhoods at a cost as low as one-tenth what slum dwellers without such systems now pay to water carriers and vendors. Sanitation systems that minimize water pollution and facilitate resource recovery have been installed in Third World cities at a cost one-twentieth that of conventional sewer systems.

Development strategies that attack poverty by emphasizing employment growth, small-scale, decentralized, quick-yielding investment programs, and wide access to land, credit, technology, and other resources have resulted in faster overall growth in per capita income as well as more rapid elimination of poverty. A more equitable distribution of arable land and more attention to smallholder agriculture typically result in higher agricultural productivity, as well as greater rural employment, wider availability of food crops, and less pressure on marginal lands and forests.

Watershed protection programs that introduce appropriate mixed-farming systems to hilly areas—checking soil erosion by maintaining continuous vegetative cover and better water control and by improving animal husbandry—afford high economic returns in the form of improved productivity and income on upland farms. Watershed reclamation projects in the Indian foothills of the Himalayas yielded a direct economic benefit-cost ratio of 2.5 to 1 and reduced sediment transport downstream by 90 percent. Similar projects in Nepal raised the incomes of participating farmers fourfold in three years. The total returns of such projects, including reductions in downstream siltation and flooding, are even more favorable.[3]

Energy conservation investments, despite the substantial gains that have already been made in many areas, remain the least-cost means to meet demands for additional energy services, even before the environmental benefits of conservation approaches are calculated. For example, a recent detailed study of the options for meeting energy demands in the U.S. Pacific Northwest through the end of this century found that the least-cost approach would be a combination of residential and industrial conservation investments and expansion of renewable energy sources (low-head

3. John Spears and Edward Ayensu, "Forest Resources," in Repetto, ed., *The Global Possible* (1985).

hydroelectric potential), which would save $2.7 billion—15 percent of the cost of meeting demands through the best conventional supply program—and eliminate the need for any additional conventional capacity.[4]

Numerous studies of the world's fisheries have demonstrated that the present catch or a greater sustainable catch could be achieved at less than half the present cost, if the overcrowding associated with inadequate restrictions on fishing was eliminated. This finding is representative of those on many common-property resources, including rangelands, forested areas, and groundwater, which are exploited beyond their optimal sustainable yield and used inefficiently with significant excess costs.

Maintaining environmental quality through pollution abatement could cost much less. In the industrial countries, estimates of the savings that can be achieved just by mechanisms that assign more of the abatement to sources that can reduce damage to the environment at lower cost typically amount to 40 to 60 percent of the present costs of pollution control. However, the longer-run savings that can be achieved by combining and changing processes to reduce and recycle wastes instead of treating and discharging them are even more significant. One innovative company, 3M, of St. Paul, Minnesota, in the past decade has reformulated products and redesigned processes to eliminate—*each year*—more than 90,000 tons of air pollutants, 10,000 tons of water pollutants, a million gallons of waste water, and 150,000 tons of solid wastes. In so doing, 3M has generated an estimated total savings for the company of about $200 million, of which 60 percent represents annual operating and maintenance costs.

Therefore, economic factors do not block the attainment of a more desirable and sustainable future—they favor it. The payoffs of better management of resources are large. The present costs of better policies and programs are small, relative to the subsequent costs or the damages to be undergone, if action is not taken. The industrial world is now finding that the costs of properly disposing of hazardous wastes or recycling them is small relative to the

---

4. A. P. Sanghvi, "Least-Cost Energy Strategies for Power System Expansion," *Energy Policy* 12, no. 1 (March 1984): 75–93.

costs of cleaning up contaminating sites of hazardous wastes later on. The developing world is now finding that the costs of watershed protection are small, relative to the costs of increased flooding and reduced irrigation and hydroelectric capacity that result from unprotected watersheds.

This advantage is multiplied by the complementary actions that promote better resource management and more sustainable development. Promoting more rapid demographic transition reduces pressures on marginal agricultural lands as well as on cities in developing countries. Actions that promote energy conservation also reduce risks of global climate change, major sources of air and water pollution, and pressures on forested areas in the Third World. Actions that encourage reforestation and protection of forested areas provide an important renewable energy source and contribute to climate regulation and to soil and water management. The elements of a program to promote sustainable development support each other and are both environmentally and economically attractive.

CHAPTER THREE

Five Ways to Use Resources Wisely

Strategies to deal with the range of resource, environmental, demographic, and economic issues that will strongly influence the attainment of a desirable future turn out to have key elements in common. There are a relatively small number of mechanisms that can be widely applied to particular situations and that yield enormous benefits over time. These mechanisms are neither speculative nor utopian; rather, they are tested and effective. Five of these key elements stood out prominently in the findings of the Global Possible Conference.

ATTENDING TO BASICS

Many problems of resource deterioration, environmental decay, population growth, and inadequate living standards persist or worsen not because they are insoluble or difficult to solve but because they have not yet been seriously addressed. One reason for this neglect is that those immediately affected have little voice, power, or economic standing. Thus, they have little ability to attract resources or attention. Yet their problems affect everybody. Poverty and lack of opportunity or choice are two of the root causes of rapid population growth, of migration to overcrowded cities, of wretched housing and environmental conditions that spread disease, of encroachment on marginal soils and forests, of depletion of coastal and inland fisheries, and of other resource pressures.

Ingenuity and resources have been lavishly applied to solve the problems and meet the needs of the world's powerful, and stunning advances have resulted. Little has been done to solve the problems and meet the needs of the urban and rural poor, the landless and marginal farmers, pastoral people and forest dwellers, or Third World women. As a result, rapid advances are still to be made at relatively low cost.

A striking example was announced recently (*Washington Post*, August 3, 1984). A team of scientists is close to developing a vaccine for malaria, a disease that is resurgent throughout the world as the *Anopheles* mosquito develops resistance to DDT and other insecticides. Malaria afflicts more than two hundred million people each year and kills millions—including a million children in Africa every year. The total cost of the research, much of which was supported by the U.S. Agency for International Development (USAID), has been about $35 million during the past twenty years. This cost, amortized over the lives likely to be saved during the next twenty years as a result of the vaccine, is probably less than a dollar per life.

The opportunities for improving resource management, environmental quality, and standards of living through low-cost and simple programs that address neglected needs of neglected populations are enormous. Low-cost health and family planning programs, emphasizing basic services and preventive care, can reduce mortality rates and raise contraceptive use rates by a factor of two within five years. Such demonstrations as the Jamkhed Rural Health Project in India and many others have obtained these results by providing the surrounding community with prenatal and postnatal care that promotes breast-feeding and monitors infant growth; contraceptive supplies and counseling; immunization against tetanus, measles, diphtheria, typhoid and tuberculosis; oral rehydration of diarrhea victims; and supplies of simple antibiotics against infection.[1] These programs do not require medical

---

1. James Grant, *The State of the World's Children, 1984* (New York: UNICEF, 1984).

specialists or expensive equipment and are affordable even in the poorest of villages. Yet half the population of the developing world outside China is still without ready access to these services.

In the poorer neighborhoods of Third World cities, now in appalling condition, safe drinking water, toilets, and washing facilities can be provided, drainage can be improved, and walks and entry roads can be constructed for modest sums. In Indonesia's Kampung Improvement Program and elsewhere, it has been demonstrated that communities will contribute rights-of-way and sites for facilities, will assess themselves to compensate households whose property is impaired, and will pay for the maintenance of water sources. Further, it has been demonstrated that much of the investment cost can be quickly recovered in higher urban property values and tax revenues. Yet the large majority of Third World urban residents live in unimproved slums and shantytowns.

Highly successful programs in rural areas of India, China, and elsewhere have greatly improved the prospects of landless and marginal farmers by allotting them seedlings, plots of deforested wasteland, and credit to enable them to plant trees. Often, the cash return per acre of those plantations has been higher than the cash return of cropland, and—at the same time—erosion and further deforestation have been checked. Yet the rate of fuelwood planting must be increased fivefold over present levels if the acute shortage of fuelwood and fodder in many Third World countries is to be relieved.

Small credit programs, which often amount to little more than easing government regulations over the interest rates that private banks can pay for deposits and charge for loans and infusing a small initial sum of capital, have freed low-income people starved for capital from the need to borrow from moneylenders at interest rates of 10 to 20 percent per month and have greatly expanded their earnings opportunities. So starved for capital are the poor in many countries that, even at interest rates 1 to 2 percent per month above inflation, borrowers can quickly expand their small-scale production or trading activities and markedly raise their earnings, expanding their credit lines and permitting the small credit institution also to expand quickly from deposits and retained earnings.

As these examples show, given a chance, the neglected will manage to help themselves. In the cities, almost all of the construction and improvement of the housing stock is through self-help and private improvement. In Bogota, Colombia, 60 percent of the neighborhoods in the city have evolved from illegal squatter settlements. Yet in many countries, the poorest in urban areas are regarded as illegal entrants. Their property rights over the shelters they build are not recognized, and their efforts to upgrade them are frustrated by authorities reluctant to acknowledge them as permanent residents. Extensive field research suggests that often mere legitimation of their presence and removal of impediments to their efforts, such as unrealistic building codes, can result in substantial improvements.

In the rural areas, credit, extension services, and infrastructure have been directed to larger farmers and prime lands, despite the evidence that yields per acre and employment per acre are usually no lower—and are often higher—on smallholdings. The training-and-visit system, which has helped extension services reach smaller farmers, has resulted in impressive gains in agricultural yields and farm incomes. In the Seyhan project in Turkey, within three years after the introduction of the training-and-visit system, farmers had increased cotton yields from 1.7 to more than 3 tons per hectare. In India, farmers in regions where the system was introduced had, within two years, raised paddy yields from 2.1 to 3 tons per hectare and wheat yields from 1.3 to nearly 2 tons per hectare. In the main, the recommendations that led to these improvements were simple, low-cost steps that were well within farmers' capabilities; better seedbed preparation and stand densities, more careful weed control, and so on.[2]

Exploiting these opportunities involves changes in approach for development agencies. There is a tendency for development agencies, both national and international, to devote the bulk of available personnel and resources to large discrete projects. Since commitments to these tend to grow as cost and time overruns occur, smaller-scale programs are disproportionately squeezed

2. Daniel Benor, *Training and Visit Extension* (Washington, D.C.: World Bank, 1984).

and other opportunities are overlooked. Large water resource projects are undertaken, whereas much more cost-effective alternatives involving rehabilitating and upgrading existing systems,
exploiting opportunities for small-scale irrigation and power development, and more efficient use of existing water resources are
neglected. Major energy development projects are undertaken,
whereas least-cost opportunities for energy conservation, cogeneration, and other small-scale decentralized energy developments
are neglected.

Correcting the balance first of all involves decentralizing more
responsibility for program planning, finance, and execution, since
no central agency can effectively develop the information required
to plan and execute a program of many small components. This,
in turn, implies greater reliance on markets for resource allocation
rather than on administrative decisions, since the latter inevitably
favor large projects and large constituents. Second, it implies involvement of community organizations to a greater degree, since
many effective programs to aid the neglected depend on community action and participation. Third, and above all, it requires
a change in priorities that puts emphasis on exploring least-cost
options and extending basic services to all before providing more
elaborate services to the better off.

MANAGING COMMON RESOURCES

The following report by Richard Witkin is excerpted from a recent
newspaper article:

> At Kennedy International Airport one recent day, 63 planes
> were scheduled to arrive in the hour beginning at 3:45 P.M.,
> but the most the airport could handle, even with clear weather,
> was 44. At Laguardia, 80 airline arrivals and departures have
> been scheduled for the hour starting at 8 A.M. on the average
> weekday. The capacity is 68. . . . These and other examples
> from the Federal Aviation Administration indicate [oversched-
> uling] is a fairly widespread problem [and has] contributed to
> a sharp rise in flight delays.
> Officials at several airlines acknowledged that they sched-

uled more rush-hour flights than the system could handle, saying they were responding to competitive pressures. There are no government controls on how many flights may be put in the airline schedule.

"If we shy away from a 5 P.M. take-off, others won't, and they'll gobble up the prime time business," said Jerry Cosley, a spokesman for Trans World Airlines (*Washington Post*, August 6, 1984).

This report aptly illustrates a much larger and more widespread need: the need to manage community resources, or common-property resources, more efficiently. In this instance, the resource is airport capacity at peak hours, to which all airlines have virtually open access, since the Federal Aviation Administration (FAA) has withdrawn from regulating schedules and routes. The result, to be expected in such conditions, is that airlines add flights until any advantage to passengers of a prime-time schedule is canceled by the probability of inconvenient delays. No airline, as Mr. Cosley rightly points out, has any rational reason to cut back on overscheduling. No airline is individually motivated to reduce the number of peak-hour flights, since the reduction in delays benefits mainly the passengers of other airlines.

This is a classic common-property problem. The inefficiency of the situation is obvious: Thousands of travelers every day suffer delays until any advantage of flying at the preferred hour is negated. The possible remedies are also classic. Schedules could be regulated by the FAA, as they were, albeit inefficiently, in the past. Landing fees could be raised for peak-hour arrivals and departures until demand no longer exceeded capacity: the economist's favorite congestion tax solution. Or permits to land could be awarded to airlines according to some fair formula, in numbers equal to airport capacity, and made tradable among them. With a sufficient number of airlines in the running, trading would lead to an eventual reallocation of landing rights that allowed the available capacity to be used efficiently and provided compensation to airlines that relinquished their rights.

The gains that can be realized from application of this mechanism for managing a common-property resource are well illustrated by Alaska's recent success in limiting entry to its salmon and herring fisheries. Without effective controls, the fate of fisheries is essentially the same as that of airports. Fishing boats crowd in, sharing the catch, until the unit costs of fish caught are as high as their average value and all profits are exhausted. In fisheries, however, the crowding often results in a catch greater than the reproductive capacity of the fishery, leading—especially in bad fishing years—to serious depletion or even exhaustion of the resource.

In the past decade, Alaska has implemented a system that awarded a limited number of fishing permits for specific fisheries (defined by region, prey, and fishing method) to individuals, based on a complex and long-negotiated formula that seeks to balance various interests. These permits are freely transferable. Although the system is by no means perfect, the results have been striking:[3]

- Since the big processors can no longer refuse to deal with fishermen who demand higher prices for their catch and encourage others to take their places, fishermen's bargaining position and the prices they receive have improved.
- Since limited entry protects fishermen from the erosion of profit margins through overcrowding, banks have been willing to provide credit to permit-holders to finance vessel improvements and gear, and fishermen have been willing to make those investments.
- Profit margins and the incomes of participating fishermen have risen. The clearest indication has been the rise in the price of permits. In the years 1976 to 1978, the price of Bristol Bay salmon gill net licenses rose from $2,000 to $25,000, and the current price is in the vicinity of $125,000. These prices reflect the capitalized value of the expected net revenues from the fisheries, values that under open access are eliminated.
- About 3 percent of permits have changed hands each year, indicating a gradual reallocation from those who, for one

3. A. Adasiak, "Alaska's Experience with Limited Entry," *Journal of the Fisheries Research Board of Canada* 36, no. 7 (1979), 770–781.

reason or another, cannot use the permits effectively to those who can.

- Fishermen have been willing to assess themselves collectively for contributions to expand hatcheries in the state, knowing that they and not some newcomer will reap the benefits of their contributions.

Unfortunately, the management of the world's common resources still resembles the situation at Laguardia airport more than that in Bristol Bay. The exploitation of renewable resources, such as groundwater, rangelands, forests, and fisheries is under virtually open access in much of the world, with serious depletion and inefficient use of the resource as the result. The use of the atmosphere, oceans, and other bodies of water as receptacles for waste products is almost entirely unlimited in much of the world, resulting in serious risks to the environment and human welfare. Resources of global scope, such as climate and the store of genetic information in the world's biological diversity, are the least effectively governed.

Consequently, there is great scope for improvement in the management of these resources, often through mechanisms similar to those used in Alaska. Where feasible, the creation or clarification of rights to the use of the resource is a powerful mechanism. Oyster grounds in Connecticut that are leased to individuals are ten times as productive as those in Maryland that are fished in common, because on individually leased beds, fishermen will seed with shellfish spat for higher yields, thin and transplant the growing crop, take steps to eliminate predators, and make other improvements. Oystermen on public waters do not, because the returns are not assured. The world harvest of aquaculture products could be expanded thirtyfold or more, if constraints on the leasing of coastal areas could be overcome and investment opportunities realized.

When permits to dispose of wastes in a public place must be purchased or when the disposer is liable for any damages that result, the firm finds ways to reduce the volume and toxicity of the wastes that need disposal. Villagers who ruthlessly cut trees for firewood and fodder in government forests will zealously nurture and protect groves that belong to them or—if community organization is sufficiently strong—to their village. Community systems of common-resource management are often highly adaptive and resilient and, too often, are undermined by development efforts rather than strengthened.

The power of these mechanisms is that they create incentives for better resource use, as they induced fishermen in Alaska to expand hatcheries and invest in better gear. Over time, these incentives foster the innovation that is required for sustainable development. Contrast the enormous resources devoted to the bioengineering of new or synthetic organisms, which are patentable and can be marketed for profit, with the meager amounts spent on the discovery of useful properties in the millions of unexplored naturally occurring species, which in general are not. From an individual standpoint, it makes sense to develop ways of conserving a resource or expanding its supply only if the benefits can be appropriated through the enforcement of property rights.

The functioning of government agencies in managing common resources can be greatly improved. In most developing countries, by and large, the mechanisms of control are just being forged to manage resources that fall naturally into the public domain: air quality, water resources, biological diversity, and fragile and unique ecosystems. Legal and administrative frameworks, the underpinnings of environmental sciences, and trained personnel are slowly being put in place, while these common resources deteriorate from overuse and mismanagement. International cooperation in strengthening the capacities of the developing countries for more effective resource and environmental management would be highly productive.

At the same time, in many developing countries, governments are straining to manage assets that could be well managed within appropriate incentive structures by private enterprises. Government forestry departments are operating plantations on lands perfectly suitable for private industrial forestry, while unique forest ecosystems are inadequately protected and lost through encroachment and while watersheds so steep and erodible that they should be under protective cover remain in the hands of individual farmers. State-owned factories and power stations, which probably would be better managed in private hands, contribute substantially to the pollution of air and water, while too little government personnel and budget are allocated to devise and implement effective systems of air and water quality protection.

In the industrial countries, governments have reacted to the pervasive environmental impacts of economic activities piecemeal with ad hoc and inefficient systems after the costs have become obvious. Pollution control has focused on abatement rather than resource recovery and recycling, and rational resource use is impeded by a thicket of fiscal and administrative measures that distort private incentives. Rationalization of these policies can yield large returns. Further, in the industrial societies, new problems of multimedia pollution, such as long-distance transport of atmospheric emissions that affect water bodies and soils, and of risks from chronic exposure to multiple toxic substances through many exposure routes, pose fundamental challenges to single-substance, single-medium, control approaches. The advantages of waste reduction through recycling and more efficient technologies for dispersal, dilution, storage, or treatment of wastes are increasingly apparent.

International agreements and institutional mechanisms can be developed to manage international common resources more effectively. Threats of climate change, depletion of the ozone shield, impoverishment of marine ecosystems, and damage to other international resources are real. The limited successes achieved to date in the Regional Seas agreements promoted by the United Nations Environment Program (UNEP), in international conventions to protect the Antarctic, to regulate trade in endangered species, and to limit ocean pollution show that there are potential positive-sum agreements from which all parties can gain but that better assessment of costs and risks and better mechanisms for creating enforceable agreements are required.

PROPER RESOURCE PRICING

The most widespread opportunity to improve resource management is also the most obvious: to treat scarce resources as if they were scarce, not as if they were free, by pricing them at the cost of increasing their supply. Competitive markets do so, signaling buyers not to devote resources to uses that have values less than the cost of supply, signaling producers to expand supplies if they can find ways to do so more efficiently, and signaling innovators to devise substitutes that can provide equivalent services more cheaply.

The most convincing demonstration in recent years of the power of pricing to affect resource use was made by the Organization of Petroleum Exporting Countries (OPEC), who combined to restrict output and raise prices dramatically. The results on energy production and use are well known. In the United States, total energy consumption fell by 2 percent between 1972 and 1983 even though gross national product rose in constant prices by more than 30 percent. The overall efficiency of energy use, therefore, has risen by one-third over the past decade. Gains in other industrial countries are of similar magnitude.

Much of this gain in efficiency has been achieved at remarkably low cost. In the household sector, the big improvements have resulted from better insulation, weatherstripping, and temperature controls that reduce the amount of energy needed for space heating and cooling. In industry, half the gains came from simple housekeeping measures, such as keeping the warehouse door closed and the furnace in better adjustment. Further improvements from more energy-efficient equipment and process designs will continue to accrue for decades as new equipment replaces old.

Equally impressive have been the power of pricing and other economic incentives to induce innovation and investment in substitutes. Since the rise in oil prices, production of solar collectors in the United States has risen by 30 percent per year, from 1.2 million to 16.8 million square feet, and three out of five new houses embody passive solar collectors. Shipments of photovoltaic generators rose from nil at the time of the first oil crisis to 5.7 megawatts in 1982 and more than tripled, to 18.5 megawatts, by 1984. Installed capacity of wind energy systems rose from 3 megawatts in 1980 to 300 megawatts in 1983 and an estimated 800 megawatts by the end of 1984. The use of energy derived from biomass fuels—primarily wood pellets, ethanol, and methanol—is increasing by 10 percent per year.

Thus, proper resource pricing is a powerful mechanism to induce more efficient production and use. The potential for further gains from pricing reform is enormous. In the United States, electric utilities are beginning to introduce rate structures that charge customers more for electricity consumed during the hours of peak demand, which requires that old, high-cost generating equipment must be brought on-line or that new, more expensive capacity must be added. In France, where "time-of-day" rates have been used since 1957, the electricity system's load factor has risen by 1.5 percent per year as customers have adapted to reduce electricity use during peak hours, and the need for sixty-five hundred megawatts in additional capacity has been avoided—15 percent of total installed capacity.

Similarly, in the use of water resources, pricing reform can result in large savings and improvements in efficiency. Throughout the world, irrigation water—which accounts for 80 percent or more of all consumptive uses—is supplied at highly subsidized rates. Federal water projects in the United States and government surface water projects in India and Pakistan, for example, both price irrigation water to farmers as much as 90 percent below the cost of storage and conveyance. In all three countries, this discourages simple conservation measures, like the lining of channels to prevent seepage (which also contributes to waterlogging and salinity) and more careful water application. Pilot projects in Pakistan have demonstrated that water losses of 40 to 60 percent in channels could be readily eliminated, and farm yields could be maintained with on-farm applications 40 percent lower if simple improvements, such as field leveling, were undertaken. In Israel, where water scarcity has forced the government to adopt a strict conservation strategy and all irrigation water is metered, allocated, and priced at increasing block rates, agricultural growth averaged 6.8 percent per year over the decade 1968 to 1978, whereas water used per hectare of irrigated land fell 21 percent. Israeli farmers are world leaders in the adoption of drip irrigation and computer-controlled systems that lead to increased crop yields and improve water-use efficiency as much as 30 percent.[4]

4. U.S. Congress, Office of Technology Assessment, *Water-Related Technologies for Sustainable Agriculture in Arid/Semi-Arid Lands* (Washington, D.C., 1983).

Conservation, more efficient irrigation practices, and the use of water on more valuable crops all result from more rational pricing. A large body of research demonstrates that each 10 percent rise in the price of water generates about 6 percent savings in water use.

Since in many countries the price of water to most agricultural users is only a small fraction of its supply cost, the scope for conservation is clearly large. In countries as diverse as India and the United States, more irrigation capacity already exists than would be needed to meet all domestic and export agricultural demands, if the efficiency of water use and the productivity of these irrigated lands attained a level near their potential.

Elsewhere in the agricultural sector, pricing reforms can powerfully assist more rational resource use. Many developing countries heavily subsidize pesticides for agricultural use, in part to encourage farmer adoption of a new technology, in part to offset policies that keep agricultural output prices artificially low. In a sample of developing countries, subsidy rates from 30 to 97 percent of full cost were recorded. As a result, farmers already familiar with the use of pesticides use them more frequently and liberally than needed, endangering the health of farm workers and accelerating the emergence of pesticide-resistant pest strains and new kinds of secondary pest problems. Pakistan, which has reduced these subsidies, encourages more rational use on the farm and eliminates a budgetary drain to make resources available for research and extension programs on safer and more effective pest management methods.

In the forestry sector, subsidies to timber operations, ranching, agricultural settlement projects, and other land uses that exploit or compete with forests are subsidized in many countries, through tax concessions, cheap credits, and reduced fees and royalty requirements for use of public lands. These subsidies shift the margin of commercially profitable exploitation of forest land far beyond what would prevail without government support. Studies have estimated that in the United States, an elimination of below-cost sales and leases of public forest and grazing lands would return tens of millions of acres to conservation status.

As these examples show, pricing reforms can often promote

resource conservation and more efficient resource use, can raise overall economic productivity by improving resource allocation, and can reduce budgetary drains that reduce government revenues available for more productive purposes. Further, since these subsidies on resource use typically benefit most those who control and use most of the resource, their elimination usually removes a source of inequity in the fiscal system.

DESIGNING FOR EFFICIENCY

Natural systems of production and consumption are designed for total resource recovery. All materials and energy flows balance. Some traditional agricultural systems mimic nature. The home garden on the typical tiny Javanese farmstead contains more than one hundred species of useful plants, ranging from ground creepers to tall trees. They use all available solar energy, prevent erosion by providing continuous ground cover, and—by their diversity—deter serious pest outbreaks without any pesticide use. Domestic animals feed on plant residues and insects and supply manure for the garden and to fertilize algal growth in fish ponds. These gardens are highly productive and internally balanced without supplementary inputs. From them the Javanese farm family derives 20 percent of its income at only 8 percent of its cost. Innovators in agro-forestry are learning much from such traditional systems.

By contrast, engineers usually design linear systems that grow by mining sources of primary materials and energy and depositing growing mountains of wastes. Conventional agricultural systems require heavy doses of fossil energy and chemicals and export massive amounts of topsoil and chemical and organic residues to the surrounding environment. Environmental regulations in most countries take these linear systems for granted and prescribe either "end-of-pipe" pollution control systems to treat waste products or standards limiting the permissible emissions rate. Neither approach deals successfully with the growing demands that ever-expanding linear systems put on the environment. Sustainable development requires that designs bend from the linear toward the circular. Large improvements in system efficiency result.

Advances in wastewater treatment provide an excellent example. Traditional systems reach farther and farther afield for suitable supplies of uncontaminated water supplies for cities that are growing. This water passes through kitchens, bathrooms, swimming pools, and sewers to treatment plants, where it is disinfected and solids and organic materials are removed. The water then passes on to the seas—leaving only the increasing problem of disposing of the remaining sludge.

Land treatment of wastewater uses the natural filtration of soils, the bacterial action of soil organisms, and sometimes the capability of plants to use the nutrients in wastewater directly. The quality of water that has undergone land treatment is typically equal or superior to that of effluent from tertiary treatment in conventional systems, there is no problem of sludge disposal, and organic material and minerals in the wastewater are available as nutrients to improve soil quality or stimulate plant growth. Treated water returns to aquifers or streams for reuse. Construction and operating costs compare favorably with conventional systems, and total system costs are lower. The number of land treatment systems for municipal wastes has risen rapidly in the United States, from 571 in 1972 to 1,100 in 1982. In Israel by the end of the century, more than 30 percent of the total wastewater flow will have been recycled for irrigation or industrial use.

Industrial process designers are increasingly seizing opportunities to reduce waste streams, as restrictions on disposal grow. Reformulating products, developing salable by-products from residuals, and redesigning or combining processes often reduce costs as well as wastes. Process improvements in a U.S. Goldkist poultry plant, for example, cut water use by 32 percent, reduced wastes by 66 percent, and saved $2.33 for every dollar spent on the changes.[5] Several U.S. companies are now recovering the methane generated in huge municipal landfills and selling it as industrial and residential fuel.

Britain now has its first Minister of Waste, who is responsible for making money by recycling the country's fifty-six million tons of annual household and industrial refuse. The valuable materials

5. Michael Royston, *Pollution Prevention Pays* (Oxford: Pergamon Press, 1979).

and the potential energy in these wastes are worth more than a billion dollars a year, according to a parliamentary committee of inquiry. "Waste is too often treated as rubbish," it proclaimed.

In the developing countries, resource recovery is highly economical because materials and energy costs are high relative to labor costs. Paper, glass, metals, plastics, oils, and other materials—even cigarette butts—are recovered from waste streams and recycled by networks of workers. Although often despised as scavengers, these workers raise resource productivity while they protect the environment.

Large-scale industries are also based on recovered resources. For example, private investors in Costa Rica, with the support of the Inter-American Development Bank (IDB), have developed a new industry based on the pulp that constitutes over half the weight of coffee beans and has been discarded as a polluting waste. A drying and processing plant that costs $5 million produces chemicals and animal feeds worth $4.5 million annually. In Costa Rica alone, this former waste has been transformed into a potential resource capable of yielding products worth $150 million per year.

Policy and institutional changes can support resource recovery. Most developing countries misguidedly attempt to stimulate industrialization by subsidizing raw materials through tax and duty exemptions. By making materials artificially cheap relative to capital, energy, labor, and finished products, these policies discourage materials conservation and recovery. Governments can encourage materials recovery by removing these subsidies and adopting other mechanisms to encourage industrialization. In the industrial countries, tax advantages to primary materials and energy producers can be removed with the same effects. Since secondary materials are close substitutes for virgin materials, materials demand over the long run is highly responsive to such policy changes.

BUILDING MANAGEMENT CAPABILITY

Especially in the Third World, where other concerns have had priority and capabilities are thinly spread, there are enormous gains to be realized by strengthening management capabilities for environmental protection and resource use. This involves putting in place the technical personnel, the management information systems, and the legal and administrative mechanisms to plan and guide resource use when market mechanisms under rational incentives are insufficient. The potential gains are large:

- Coastal countries lack means to manage fisheries within their Exclusive Economic Zones (EEZs). Data from which the allowable harvest could be estimated and systems to monitor and control fishing effort are absent.
- In most countries, systems to control use of groundwater are lacking: information on recharge and sustainable yield, as well as mechanisms to monitor and control withdrawals, is not available for most aquifers.
- Although many countries have adopted laws and regulations to govern pesticide use, the means to enforce them and the monitoring systems for early detection of adverse health effects, pest resistance, and secondary pest emergence are not in place.
- Although master plans and land use plans have been drawn up in Third World cities, the implementation of zoning regulations is deficient.
- The management of urban services such as solid waste collection is poor, leading to deteriorating environmental quality and affecting water quality and drainage.
- Although reserved forests and conservation areas have been demarcated, the means to control the use of these areas by individuals and by commercial interests often are undeveloped, as is the ecological knowledge for sustained multiple use.

In these circumstances, much can be accomplished by attention to management and administrative concerns. Modern data systems can make an enormous difference. Substantial gains in productivity are possible by reallocating expenditures toward maintenance and improvement of existing systems, away from new construction projects. Training, management assistance, and productivity incentives are proven tools that have wide applicability in the management of resources as well.

A powerful means to improve management is involving the people and communities that are directly affected both in the planning and implementation of programs. Overcentralized, bureaucratic processes fail to take advantage of local knowledge of needs, preferences, and opportunities—or of the managerial capabilities of local communities. Often, adversarial relationships emerge between officials and the local communities they are supposed to serve. Partnerships between the public sector and community organizations have succeeded in improving health and family planning programs, the urban environment, soil conservation and watershed protection, community forestry, and other resource programs.

CONCLUSION

These mechanisms are not the only effective means by which substantial improvements in future welfare and resource availability can be ensured. The application of research and technology to critical world problems, better monitoring of resource and environmental conditions, the awakening of public opinion, and political action are also important—many would say more important. The availability of all these means reinforces the basic theme of this book, that ample opportunities exist to build a prosperous and sustainable future.

The many projections and assessments underlying the Global Possible project papers have in common a widening range of outcomes, as the point of reference moves ahead into the next century. These increasingly divergent futures reflect primarily the consequences of different policy choices. Decisions taken now are critical because of the momentum built into the processes of global change. It is the awareness of the tremendous long-term benefits that follow from relatively small and simple steps that creates a sense of optimism about the global possible.

CHAPTER FOUR

Applications to Specific Resources

POPULATION, RESOURCE PRESSURES, AND POVERTY

Births, deaths, and population growth rates have dropped dramatically in China and many other developing countries, and the world's population growth rate has turned down. Yet the poorest nations and less modernized parts of other countries still face population doublings every generation, exploding cities, and enormous momentum for future growth. The medium U.N. projection implies a world population of 6.1 billion by the year 2000, 8.2 billion in 2025, and 10.2 billion when population stops increasing at the end of the next century. Only about 10 percent of these additional people will live in today's rich countries.

Like all extrapolations, the United Nation's (U.N.) population projection runs the risk of missing important turning points. Post-World War II projections missed the baby boom and sharp improvements in Third World life expectancy; later projections missed the downturn in fertility. If the world reaches the two-child family required for eventual stability just twenty years earlier than the United Nations assumes, world population will settle down at about 8 billion, more than 2 billion people fewer than the medium projection. On the other hand, if replacement levels of fertility are reached only twenty years later than projected, more than 2.5 billion more people will be added to the ultimate world population. This swing is as large as the global population today. What happens during the rest of this century will profoundly affect the lives our descendants will know. Population growth as fast as the United Nations foresees cannot help but intensify economic, resource, and environmental pressures in the Third World.[1]

Countries in every hemisphere and at every income level that have taken the steps described in this chapter have reduced birth and death rates relatively quickly: Cuba, China, Korea, Sri Lanka, Thailand—are all very different countries but all have been successful in speeding up the demographic transition. This demonstrates that the more optimistic projection is feasible and attainable. If all countries take similar steps, world population can stabilize in the next century before it doubles again.

Perhaps a fourth of the world's inhabitants now live in what the World Bank calls "absolute poverty,"—with poor health, undernutrition, chronic deprivation, and shortened life expectancy. These people consume a tiny share, less than 5 percent, of the world's output, whereas the fourth of the world's population in the rich countries consumes more than two-thirds. The human suffering and waste implicit in these numbers is one of the great tragedies of the modern era. Widespread poverty perpetuates high birth and death rates.[2] Moreover, the enormous worldwide resource demands of the rich countries and the pressures of necessity on the poor's limited resources are steadily eroding the resource base that must sustain a much larger population in the future.[3]

Strong efforts are needed to reduce world poverty and thereby to create the conditions for accelerated declines in fertility and mortality. Countries such as Korea that have succeeded in this

1. World Bank, *World Development Report, 1984* (Oxford: Oxford University Press, 1984). See also Robert S. McNamara, "Time Bomb or Myth: The Population Problem," *Foreign Affairs* 62, no. 5 (Summer 1984): 1107–31.

2. Robert Repetto, *Economic Equality and Fertility in Developing Countries* (Baltimore: Johns Hopkins University Press for Resources for the Future, 1979). Samuel H. Preston, "Causes and Consequences of Mortality Declines in Less Developed Countries during the Twentieth Century," in Richard Easterlin, ed., *Population and Economic Change in Developing Countries* (Chicago: University of Chicago Press for the National Bureau of Economic Research, 1980).

3. Robert Repetto and Thomas Holmes, "The Role of Population in Resource Depletion in Developing Countries," *Population and Development Review* 9, no. 4 (December 1983).

despite scant resources and dense populations demonstrate that commitment, appropriate policies, and international support will rapidly reduce poverty and population growth.

Most households in those Third World countries where birth and death rates are still high do not have ready access to basic health and family planning services. Consequently, tens of millions die each year of easily preventable or curable illness, and perhaps a hundred million unplanned conceptions lead to unwanted births or abortions. If these basic services are widely extended to poor households in need, especially in rural areas, these shocking figures can be changed.

The experience of countries where birth and death rates have fallen rapidly shows that two mutually reinforcing strategies are effective. First, services that provide basic health care and contraceptive supplies and information must be accessible to almost all households. Second, broad-based economic and social development must change the conditions that perpetuate high fertility and mortality rates. Both require a strong government commitment to the welfare of the people.

As people often speak of "husbanding" resources, the fact that women are the ultimate guardians of family health and the resources needed for survival is often overlooked. Providing more social, economic, and educational opportunities for women leads not only to lower birth rates but also to better health and nutrition—especially for babies and children. In many countries, the women grow the subsistence crops and raise small animals, gather wood and water for the family's use, and provide much of the cash income through trading and handicrafts. Yet women are usually neglected, and sometimes held back, by development programs.

Lowering birth and death rates, alleviating poverty, improving women's opportunities, and reducing resource pressures are highly complementary. When half a country's deaths are those of infants and children younger than five, many closely spaced births result in high infant mortality, which in turn weakens parents' motivation to plan their families. Poverty and population growth reinforce each other. Measures to alleviate poverty will favorably affect women's opportunities, and vice versa, and rising incomes make improved environmental standards affordable.

The most essential and powerful way to draw people out of

poverty is to accelerate job creation, particularly for unskilled and semiskilled workers. Most poor people are in the labor force and have nothing but their labor to sell. Their earnings are limited by the lack of productive jobs. For the rest of this century, the Third World's labor force will increase faster than its total population. In many countries, most new workers—especially women workers—are being forced into overcrowded, low-paying service jobs in the cities or have too little farm work in the countryside. Unless jobs are created more rapidly, their earnings will not increase.

Using more labor wherever warranted also reduces resource and environmental pressures by reducing energy and materials inputs per unit of output. There are broad opportunities for substituting labor for power equipment and raw materials, both in the mix of commodities that are produced and the techniques that are used to produce them.

Some of the straightforward steps that Third World governments can take to accelerate job creation involve pricing scarce resources as if they were scarce; others involve attending to basics. They can raise capital and energy costs and interest rates to realistic levels to discourage excessive use of capital. They can direct a larger share of development funds toward dispersed, small-scale programs that employ more labor and provide quicker returns than larger-scale, capital-intensive programs. They can reduce trade restrictions that unduly protect internal markets and discourage exports, which are often relatively labor-intensive.

Governments of industrial countries can support these efforts while promoting higher productivity at home by reducing quantitative restrictions on labor-intensive manufactures from the Third World, simplifying import procedures, and compensating and retraining workers displaced by imports instead of relying on trade restraints. Dismantling protective barriers controls domestic inflation and spurs productivity growth, but it is nearly impossible if macroeconomic policies keep exchange rates far from levels that balance foreign trade, as the U.S. dollar exchange rate is now. Governments of industrial countries can also eliminate the escalation of tariff rates on processed materials so that developing countries are not deterred from processing their export commodities. These steps are "positive-sum," because both importing and exporting countries are better off when the scope for international trade increases.

Of equal importance are international capital flows, which create more jobs in the receiving country and yield high returns. Unfortunately, official capital flows for development purposes to low-income countries through bilateral and multilateral channels, such as the International Development Association, are under extreme pressure, just when private flows are also shrinking. Virtually every dollar transferred to Third World countries returns to the industrial countries to pay for additional imports or to service existing debt. The usefulness of the official flows that do continue can be raised by further expanding the share transferred through program and structural adjustment lending linked not to the purchase of equipment but to the pursuit of appropriate programs and policies. Private flows can be encouraged by spreading and reducing the risks of investing in low-income countries, by co-financing projects, expanding insurance facilities, and creating more financial intermediaries.

In addition to these employment-generating policies, development programs that attend to basics by building from the bottom up can make much more rapid inroads on poverty. Most development programs serve the urban elite, neglecting the poor—especially the rural poor. If public funds provide a basic level of services for virtually all and the better-off are required to pay for the superior services they enjoy, this situation can be reversed. This may sound simple, but it involves reexamining and reordering expenditure priorities in virtually every budget sector. It also entails raising user charges and other cost recovery mechanisms to cover marginal costs, especially in programs that serve mainly the middle- and upper-income groups, and limiting the use of public subsidies except in programs directed toward the very lowest income groups. Too often public services are provided almost free but do not reach poor people who must rely on them most.

Population pressures on resources usually reflect an extremely skewed distribution of resources. When farmers encroach on tropical forests or cultivate erodible hillsides, population pressure is blamed, but the pressure typically stems from the concentration of land in large holdings. The smallest 50 percent of farms typically amount to less than 5 percent of the total cropped area. If pressures on marginal lands are to be reduced, better lands must be used more intensively. In many countries, large farmers control much of the better land and do not use it as intensively as small farmers who have adequate access to credit, other inputs, and extension services. In these countries, agrarian reform and greater attention to small farmers would do much to alleviate poverty, raise employment, and reduce pressure on marginal soils.

Although agrarian reform is perhaps the most sensitive and politically difficult of all development programs, it does not necessarily mean a bloody land redistribution, and there are a wide variety of measures that point in the right direction. Many current agricultural development programs actually promote *greater* land concentration by benefiting large farmers disproportionately, although smaller farmers can hold their own in fair competition. If research programs include smallholder crops, if extension programs are designed to reach the small farmer, if agricultural prices are not manipulated, and if small farmers have equal access to credit and other inputs, they will not lose ground in the marketplace. Almost always, small farmers get a better deal in straight commercial dealings than from subsidized programs that create artificial scarcities and require complicated administrative procedures.

Small farmers often hold scattered plots that can be leveled, drained, and irrigated more easily in blocks. Such land improvements, combined with plot consolidation, are good investments, especially if farms are surveyed and tenures registered at the same time. But this can only be carried out with government involvement. With secure tenures, however, small farmers will work harder to raise productivity. If rural credit agencies are able to provide financing, their access to land can be increased through compensated redistributions or private sales and leases.

Governments that have tried to implement far-reaching agrarian reform have typically been revolutionary, and often socialist or Marxist in ideology. Therefore, the capitalist world has been suspicious or downright hostile, despite the importance of successful Western-sponsored land reforms in such capitalist countries as Japan, Taiwan, and Korea to those countries' subsequent development. Strong and consistent support from the capitalist world for agrarian reform programs, even if tinged with socialist ideology, would be enormously helpful. The record of the communist and socialist countries makes abundantly clear that private enterprise has little to fear from collectivism in the countryside.

Not only physical resources, but also human resources, can be developed more equitably. Many countries have made the changes in the school system and the workplace that provide women with greater opportunities. Even Libya, not otherwise a beacon of enlightenment, has achieved universal primary education for women and markedly raised enrollment rates in secondary schools and colleges. Strong public support for women's educational and social advancement can be reinforced by such measures as building more primary and junior secondary schools in local communities; lowering educational costs to parents at the primary level, especially in rural areas; opening and reserving places for women in institutions that train technicians and managers for the modern economy; recruiting more women to be teachers in secondary schools and colleges; and expanding out-of-school educational programs for women who have little formal schooling.

Where job opportunities for women are expanding, girls are more likely to stay longer in school because their acquired skills pay off. Women work predominantly in agriculture and related processing industries, trade and services, and light manufacturing. If these sectors grow rapidly, women's participation increases. Since these are labor-intensive sectors, they thrive under employment-oriented development policies, and women, who disproportionately work in family enterprises, benefit if the barriers between the modern and the traditional parts of the economy are lowered. Small enterprises thrive in bazaar-like marketplaces and can be encouraged by deregulating inputs and credits, relaxing the scope of administrative licensing, and encouraging market competition.

The role of business enterprise is critical. Businesses can ensure that recruitment, training, work practice, promotion, and compensation practices actively encourage women to participate. Nongovernmental organizations (NGOs) can effectively advocate change and establish pilot programs to broaden economic opportunities for women. Legal barriers can also be lowered by revising laws and administrative procedures that impede women's advancement and by removing discrimination against women as borrowers and property owners.

All these are powerful mechanisms for solving population and poverty problems, but specific health and family planning programs also have much to contribute. Simple and well-known measures that do not cost much or require highly trained personnel can improve health and lower death rates strikingly. Both in the industrial countries and in the Third World, these gains can be realized by shifting emphasis toward health promotion and preventive measures. The United Nations International Children's Emergency Fund (UNICEF) and other agencies have pointed out the means for achieving dramatic health improvements in the Third World: oral rehydration therapy, expanded immunization programs, growth monitoring of infants, prenatal and postnatal care, and health education. These and other basic health services can be provided at an affordable cost of $2 to $4 per capita annually. Yet 75 percent of the Third World population lacks them.

Providing basic health services to all households involves a national commitment by Third World leadership to the development of primary health care for rural populations. The key is creating facilities in the villages and urban neighborhoods using paramedical personnel, with expanded outreach to households by workers recruited from the community. Given the scarcity of funds, basic health services for all can only be financed by revising inefficient health systems that overemphasize inpatient urban hospital services; that spend wastefully on supplies, drugs, and equipment; and that use physicians too much as clinical specialists rather than as public health team leaders. Medical educators everywhere can participate in changing training programs to provide many more paramedical workers and to educate physicians as public health supervisors.

Enormous savings can be realized while service is improving, as increasing numbers of countries are discovering, by reforming the drug supply system to simplify and cheapen the drug list, rationalize procurement and distribution, and make supplies available in the local community. Finally, since funding is a key issue in expanding the network of health services, the way health services are financed must be changed to ensure that those who can pay for them, do so, saving public funds to provide basic services to the poor.

Advanced country institutions can help by redirecting foreign assistance toward primary health care and away from programs using expensive technologies to serve the urban elite; redirecting training programs to support the primary health system and preventive activities; and increasing long-term funding for research on health problems that result in most of the world's sickness and death, including the diarrheal diseases, malaria, and other tropical diseases.

Providing contraceptive supplies, services, and information is a way of promoting family health and well-being, not just a birth control program. Family planning programs are more effective if they build on people's values, and they are part of an overall effort to improve people's lives. These kinds of services are badly needed. Most women who say they want no more children or want to delay their next pregnancy are not protected, partly because adequate family planning services are not readily available to them. If birth rates are to decline as rapidly as optimistic population projections imply, the number of contraceptive users must rise by at least 6.5 percent annually for the next thirty years. Expanding the availability of services at this pace requires continuing increases in funding; recruitment and training of personnel; organizational effort; and the strong support of governments, international agencies, and voluntary organizations.

Because this basic service is so important, an international goal should be set to double access to family services in the Third World over the coming decade. At the Second World Population Conference in Mexico City in 1984, the World Bank announced its doubling of support for population and health programs. Other bilateral and multilateral assistance agencies should follow suit, focusing particularly on countries where population growth rates are very high, birth rates are not declining, and poverty is widespread.

Approaches that work include using community workers to visit couples, supply contraceptives, and provide basic health services; using subsidized commercial sales of contraceptives and commercial marketing channels; using incentives to families who continue as family planners; expanding the range of birth control methods made available; and involving local governmental and nongovernmental bodies more fully in managing programs.

Restricting the availability of safe abortion services just leads to more illicit, unsafe, and often fatal abortions and more unwanted births. In Third World countries and among teenagers in the industrial countries, abortions are most frequent when adequate contraceptive protection is not available, and abortions can best be reduced by widespread contraceptive accessibility and information, including services for young people. Where not opposed by religious and moral principles, safe abortion services should be made available to those in need.

Promising new long-acting contraceptives are near the stage of widespread availability, but there is a need for continuing research—with government support, if necessary—on long-acting methods for both sexes and self-administered postcoital methods for women. Long-term health research is needed for both preliminary testing of new contraceptive products and continuing evaluation of their safety and effectiveness in Third World settings as well as in industrialized countries.

Resolving the challenge of population growth and widespread poverty among at least one-half of the world's peoples requires that development programs attend to the basics. Creating sustainable poverty-free societies will be possible only if the initiative and capacities of the people themselves are mobilized both through the marketplace and through the empowerment of citizen's groups and local organizations. In this way, the diversity of cultural values, ecological adaptations, and social responses to development challenges will find full expression.

THE URBAN ENVIRONMENT

Third World cities have been mushrooming. While rural populations doubled between 1920 and 1980, city populations grew tenfold, from one hundred million to one billion, and the largest cities have expanded at the fastest pace. By the year 2000, most of the largest metropolitan areas will be in the Third World, and almost half of the Third World population will be urban. Mexico City will have expanded from sixteen to thirty-one million, Sao Paulo from twelve to twenty-five million, and Nairobi from one to five million.

Although Latin America and East Asia are already quite urbanized and cities' growth rates have slowed somewhat, the number of new urban residents still increases every year. In South Asia and Africa, only a small fraction of the people live in cities, but growth rates will continue to be high for decades, and the numbers of new city dwellers will rise rapidly. In 1980, only 36 million Africans lived in cities of a million people or more, but by the year 2000 the number will have jumped almost fivefold, to 154 million. In these regions, where the economic base is also much lower, there are severe problems in providing urban residents with even the most basic infrastructure. In Freetown, Sierra Leone, for example, most of the lower-income households occupy shacks built on riverbanks, steep hills, refuse dumps, and other waste land. Eighty percent of households have no water tap, and 95 percent no toilet in their houses.

In almost all Third World cities, poor people live in extremely unhealthy and degraded conditions. They lack space, drinking water, sanitation, waste collection, drainage, lighting, other urban services, minimally adequate housing, and even the acknowledged right to be where they are. Their health and life expectancy are often worse than in the countryside, where fewer medical services are available. Uncontrolled pollution from industries and vehicles compound the health risks, affecting urban residents and spreading to the surrounding environment. These problems have not been widely recognized with the sense of urgency they deserve, and efforts to deal with them have been too limited to have much impact.[4]

Unless the rate of migration to the largest cities can be slowed down, it will be nearly impossible to improve housing and environmental conditions. Decentralizing industries and improving

---

4. Jorge E. Hardoy and David Satterthwaite, "Third World Cities and the Environment of Poverty," in Repetto, ed., *The Global Possible.*

living conditions and opportunities in smaller cities and rural areas will help by reducing the impetus to migrate in the first place. But natural increase accounts for a significant—and often the greater—part of the cities' growth, so controlling migration can limit the problem but cannot solve it. Slowing population growth rates through the actions discussed in the previous section will also help tremendously, especially in South Asia and Africa.

It is not surprising that city governments should be under terrible stress in countries where incomes are low and huge metropolises are burgeoning. Their problems are compounded by administrative and management deficiencies. Most city administrations have limited power over revenue sources and expenditures, since most of the spending and taxing in urban areas is controlled by national governments. They are hampered by severe shortages of trained administrators and by poor management. These deficiencies lie at the heart of the inability to deal with pressing problems. Improving the management of public transportation programs, waste collection services, urban utilities, and tax administration could make an enormous difference.[5] Chinese cities suffer from terrible air and water pollution, but the streets are swept daily and the rubbish is carted away, traffic is orderly, and vehicles are forbidden to use their horns in downtown areas. These measures are not expensive, and they certainly make the cities more livable. Absolutely essential to the long-term viability of urban centers is the development of administrative capabilities and an adequate financial base.

Probably, between a third and a half of the residents of Third World cities are living on public or private lands illegally. In Manila, a 1980 study found that 2 million of the 5.5 million inhabitants lived in illegal squatter settlements and only 15 percent of Manila's households could afford to rent or buy legal housing on the open market. Squatters are subject to instant ejection and destruction of their housing, cannot get credit, are usually ineligible for most government services, and are themselves often subject to fines or arrest. In many metropolitan areas, millions of urban poor

5. Johannes E. Linn, *Cities in the Developing World* (Washington, D.C.: World Bank, 1983).

are simply swept under the rug and wished away. Legalizing their status is an important prerequisite to any effort to improve the urban environment and urban living conditions.

Environmental conditions in Third World cities are complex, poorly understood, and daunting. There are many things that can be done, but their success depends entirely on the political will of governments to take action founded on a commitment to social justice.

The key to reducing rates of rural-to-urban migration is to modify development strategies biased against rural areas. Macro-economic policies that penalize agriculture and agriculturally-based industries, investment priorities that favor costly urban in-frastructure, and fiscal systems that transfer resources toward the urban middle class all contribute to the lack of infrastructure, opportunities, and employment in the rural areas.

The import-competing industries that arise behind protective barriers cluster around the largest cities, especially if import and investment licenses, credit, and other business permits require central approval. Export industries, often based on agricultural or other natural resources, tend to be more dispersed. Although in-dustrial location planning is important, experience shows that it is no more than doodling on a map unless it is realistic and in harmony with the incentives that guide business decisions. And businesses pay far more attention to fundamental locational ad vantages than to specific locational incentives that governments offer to offset those advantages.

The market conditions that lead to industrial concentration in and around the largest cities and the consequent population growth and environmental stress can be reduced by lessening the bias in trade policy favoring import-competing industries, as well as by relaxing administrative control over business operations. Import-competing industries naturally flock to the largest markets, and if business success depends on seeing someone in government to get import licenses, credit approvals, tax concessions, invest-ment permits, and other clearances, businessmen will surely lo-cate near the metropolis.

Urban governments must raise their revenue bases to meet growing demands for services. Although generally poor, cities have much higher incomes than rural areas and must pay their own way. Enough money can be found to provide decent services for all, but getting it requires both political determination and the cooperation of the national government. Often, the most able administrators, the most promising sources of revenue, and the authority to deal with critical problems are preempted by the central government.

Urban governments can improve their revenue performance by basing charges for urban services on incremental costs for all users able to pay them. In many cities, water and electricity rates, bus and train fares, rubbish collection charges, and other fees are far less than the costs of providing the services. As a result, huge fiscal deficits eat up revenues, service is poor, and there is no money to extend services to populations—usually poor—without any service at all. Cities can start by investing in improved metering, collection, and enforcement of charges; by improving property tax assessment and collection; and by developing innovative revenue sources.

National governments can expand revenue sharing or consider decentralizing revenue sources and administrative functions to metropolitan levels of government, and they can help build up the capabilities of urban administration. International aid agencies can also help by expanding programs of technical assistance and training to strengthen city government.

Too often, upper-income urban areas are served with expensive technologies, but low-income areas are hardly served at all. This is a problem of not attending to basics. Technologies and systems are available that can provide acceptable services cheaply and facilitate resource recovery. There are alternatives to conventional sewerage systems, for example, that foster resource recovery, conserve water, and cost one-tenth as much. Neighborhood water stands that provide safe drinking water and a place for bathing and washing clothes give low-income households an escape from polluted water sources. In Jakarta, these water stands are maintained by concessionaires who also deliver water door to door for a charge. Low-cost systems like these can be extended broadly, and the history of most cities shows that extensive upgrading takes place over time. Instead of investing in large showpiece projects, governments and aid agencies could wisely use the funds to extend basic services into poor neighborhoods; provide house sites for the growing population; and upgrade conditions in slums and shantytowns.

These programs will be more effective if it is recognized that improvements in the urban environment will take place largely through the self-help of residents. Urban administrations should support and cooperate with community groups. If shantytowns are legalized and residents are enabled to obtain secure tenures so that they may borrow for improvements and be assured of the benefits of their efforts, if unrealistic building codes and difficult procedures for getting loans and permits are eliminated, neighborhoods will pull themselves up by the bootstraps.

Much more can be done to control industrial pollution problems at reasonable cost. Typically, the polluters are losing money, not saving it, by the lack of controls. The buses and trucks that spew black smoke on Third World city dwellers would run better, use less fuel, and last longer if their engines were tuned occasionally and maintained better. Much of the fuel consumed in industrial boilers goes right up the chimney through incomplete combustion, resulting in low energy efficiency and high fuel costs. Valuable materials that could easily be recovered are dumped into rivers and canals, resulting in horrors like the mercury and cadmium poisonings that have occurred in Nicaragua, Indonesia, and elsewhere. Often, governments set unrealistic pollution standards but do not enforce them, and master plans governing land use are produced but not followed because zoning and building regulations are weak. Shantytowns grow up at factory walls, increasing the risks of disasters like that at Bhopal.

The sensible thing for urban administrators to do is to establish reasonable priorities for pollution control, starting with the supply of safe drinking water, proceeding to the enforcement of controls on large new sources, and then tackling the worst of existing sources. It makes more sense to achieve the 50-percent reduction in emissions that can usually be accomplished simply and cheaply than to insist on a theoretical 90-percent reduction that is not implemented. Almost no Third World cities with substantial industrial bases have any safe disposal facilities for toxic and hazardous wastes, which end up in rivers and landfills to cause terrible problems later on. Such facilities are a high-priority need.

Land-use planning would be much more effective if planners placed greater emphasis on strengthening the instruments of control and less emphasis on the compilation of paper plans. Tunisia and other countries have demonstrated one way to do this and generate revenues at the same time: the city buys land in advance, lays it out in industrial estates and residential sites with the appropriate infrastructure, and then resells it. This also helps in preserving open space, a crucial amenity that few Third World cities still have. But much can be done simply by better management of zoning regulations, building permits, and other instruments of urban land-use control.

There are currently no NGOs specifically focusing on human settlements, although some religious groups and secular associations are trying to come to grips with the problems. In the slums, citizens' groups, often led by women, have struggled to secure the land they occupy or to get water, sanitation, schools, and other vital services from the government. There is much that voluntary organizations in the industrial world can do to raise the awareness of these problems among governments, international agencies, and the world public. They can help by exchanging information about successful measures promoted by local groups and by publicizing that experience; encouraging the development of indicators, data-gathering methods, and reporting mechanisms to allow better monitoring of urban conditions; and developing a permanent network of cooperating and supportive citizens' groups.

Most people in the world in the next century will live in cities. Their lives can be lives of squalor and disease or lives of expanded opportunity. Cities are expensive, and the fundamental choice is between a decent environment for the many or a privileged environment for the few.

FRESH WATER RESOURCES

The good news is that there is more than enough fresh water in the world to meet current and future needs, even though much of the planet's fresh water is locked up in ice, deep lakes, and aquifers or flushes off the land in annual flood runoff or moves between sky and oceans in evaporation and rainfall that is unavailable for use. Depending on how the terms are defined, all human water uses today touch between one- and two-thirds of the fresh water readily available, although the amount used is only about 1 percent of the planet's yearly rainfall, which in turn is less than one-tenth of all the fresh water stored in the world. So in some global sense water is not scarce.[6]

The bad news is that many regions and entire countries are facing serious water shortages and that many more soon might, either because demands are growing rapidly or because their water resources are being degraded by agricultural and industrial pollution. Per unit of land area, Africa's annual runoff is only one-fifth that of South America's, and per person, Asia has only one-half the world's average availability. Furthermore, in many semi-arid regions, rainfall varies widely from year to year in largely unpredictable patterns, and droughts imperil substantial populations. Recent tragedies in Ethiopia and the Sahel prove how disastrous a few years of low rainfall can be.

Unfortunately, we do not know the extent of the bad news, because the data on water availability, quality, and use are now lacking or sadly deficient for most regions. Even for the United States, for example, the figures on the number of acres under irrigation in the mid-1970s varied from forty-one to sixty one million acres, depending on which government agency provided the estimates.

The ranchers, farmers, and miners who settled the territories of Arizona, Colorado, and New Mexico would scarcely recognize modern Tuscon or Denver or today's large-scale industries and sophisticated agricultural operations. But they would recognize the rules and laws that govern water use. Those rules were devised by the settlers and remain essentially the same today. In many other parts of the world also, considerable shifts in population, land, and water use have not been accompanied by adjustments in the laws, institutions, and policies that control water resources.

6. M. O. L'vovich, *World Water Resources and Their Future*, translation by the American Geophysical Society, 1979.

Outmoded institutions and policies constrain efficient water management, making it difficult to reallocate water from historical uses and users to new purposes, however productive. Instead, the response to growing demands has always been to find new supplies. This seems to be true in political and economic systems as different as those of the United States, the Soviet Union, China, and India.

Irrigated agriculture is by far the largest consumer of water in the world today and so it is likely to remain, even though irrigation as currently practiced in most areas uses water extremely inefficiently. In India and Pakistan, where irrigation is vital and water is scarce, 80 to 90 percent of the water diverted from rivers by many large irrigation systems is lost before it reaches the crop root zone and can do any good. The water lost through seepage out of the canals often does considerable harm by contributing to waterlogging and salinization of the surrounding soils. Large savings of water are possible from relatively small investments in irrigation technology, management, and agricultural practices. Pilot projects in Pakistan have demonstrated that water losses can easily be cut in half and that the benefits of the water can be raised substantially just by adjusting the timing of irrigation to crop needs, grading the irrigated fields more carefully, and other simple improvements.

Even though the patterns of water availability and use and the institutions that affect them vary from area to area, it is possible to identify general goals and ways of moving toward them. One important goal is greater efficiency in water use to ensure its long-term availability for high-priority uses and to minimize the dangers to human health from careless practices. Another is protection of the ecological processes and systems (including watersheds, floodplains, and the biota) through which water moves, to ensure a sustainable, secure, and safe water supply to meet human needs. These goals and many of the steps needed to achieve them specifically advance the objective of the U.N. Drinking Water and Sanitation Decade, now in its third year, to provide reasonable access to safe water to all people.

Better data on hydrological flows, water quality, and current and future water uses are fundamental if water management is to be improved. Without such data, estimating future demands and designing sensible engineering projects and management systems are impossible. The starting point for any country is an analysis of its existing fresh water uses and resources. Baseline and monitoring data on water availability, quality, and use should be collected using entire river basins as units. To help in this substantial task, international assistance organizations, which have invested huge sums in water resource development, can fund data collection systems in developing countries and help in executing water supply and demand studies.

As industries and cities grow and farms use the land and chemical inputs more intensively, demands for fresh water grow, and this resource cannot continue to be made available without cost. A scarce resource cannot be priced as if it were free. Nor can water bodies continue to be used freely for dumping all kinds of wastes. If this painful fact is ignored, water use will be inefficient, scarcities will emerge, water quality will deteriorate, and water will become a headache, not a resource. A recent case in California illustrates the point: highly subsidized irrigation water liberally used to irrigate poorly drained soils with high mineral content drained into a system of wildlife refuges and devastated the ecosystem. The final result, after the expenditure of hundreds of millions of dollars on irrigation and drainage systems, is likely to be not only their abandonment but the loss of tens of thousands of acres of farmland as well.

In the developing world, the headaches can be worse, if anything. Because rivers are used indiscriminately as dumps, water pollution is noisome and hazardous. The Hooghly River, which branches off the Ganges and passes right through Calcutta, is choked with the untreated wastes from more than 150 factories and raw sewage from more than 350 outfalls. Yet some of Calcutta's homeless bathe in it.

If the costs of the engineering projects that make water safe and available are not recovered, the systems cannot be operated or maintained properly. They cannot be replaced as needed unless their financial underpinnings are sound. Some countries, like China and the Philippines, have begun making local and provincial authorities responsible for financing water projects in their districts, including servicing and repaying loans from national and international agencies. This powerfully focuses their attention on the economic worth of the water projects they propose and strongly encourages them to put in place and enforce mechanisms to recover their costs, in turn, from the beneficiaries.

But not only are there losses to be avoided, there are also substantial gains to be realized from rational water pricing. The efficiency of water use in irrigation can be improved by as much as 50 percent with readily available cost-effective means. In Israel, where the scarcity of water is reflected in high prices and careful management, farmers plant crops that yield high returns per unit of water and achieve on-farm efficiencies of water use as great as 85 percent through precise timing and placement of water and elimination of water losses. The most effective way of promoting better water use is by pricing water to cover the full costs of supply.

Industrial water use is very sensitive to price. In the United States, for example, where almost 90 percent of industrial water use is for cooling, industries such as electric power generation can move from once-through to recirculatory to dry cooling systems as the effective price of water increases, reducing large water needs virtually to zero. With price adjustments to reflect full supply costs, tremendous improvements in water efficiency can be achieved using proven technologies. At the same time, far fewer pollutants will be released into the environment.

Even in poor urban neighborhoods, safe drinking water can be provided through well-managed community supply points at prices that cover costs and are yet affordable, often much less than poor households otherwise pay for water of inferior quality and availability. For example, in Lima, Peru, poor families were buying water from street vendors at three times the price paid by better-off households with pipe connections.

In countries where large investments in water resource development have already been made, the best sites for storage and irrigation have already been used, and enough capacity has been created to meet all demands for irrigation, if existing systems even approach their maximum productivity. If yields from irrigated land in India approached those in China, Taiwan, or the Philippines, for example, little more than half the acreage planned for irrigation would be necessary to meet all needs for agricultural production.[7] For both reasons, future investments that emphasize rehabilitation, better operation, and increased production on existing systems offer the best returns.

As many are now finding under the pressure of financial stringency, governments and aid agencies might do better to emphasize rehabilitation and improvement of older works before costly new construction is undertaken. Rehabilitation has relatively low capital costs, and farmers who have experience with irrigation quickly respond to improvements in water supplies. Among new projects, priority on new construction should generally go to smaller irrigation systems that can be locally managed and offer more scope for innovative and user-oriented design. Thailand has successfully developed a large number of small-scale irrigation projects that depend on local water users' associations for effective operation. If development agencies promote these water users' associations before construction of an irrigation project begins and involve these groups in planning and operation, the likelihood of quick and successful operation becomes much greater. Where irrigation is traditional, as in Thailand, Java, and Bali, there are historical antecedents for such water users' associations that can be revitalized to strengthen the management of small and large systems and to facilitate cost recovery.

Storing water to stabilize variations between years is essential, but too much attention has been given to surface storage. Most of the appropriate sites have been impounded, and in surface storage huge volumes of water are wasted between the point of storage and the point of use. As an alternative, attention should be directed to groundwater storage. Appropriate sites exist around the world for groundwater storage at significantly lower costs. In India's Gangetic Plain, which runs clear across the subcontinent, there are almost no suitable sites for surface storage, and much of the snowmelt from the Himalayas to the north runs off into the Bay of Bengal—flooding almost a third of Bangladesh each year on the way. As tube-well irrigation has expanded in these granary states of India, the possibility has been raised of promoting

7. Peter P. Rogers, "Fresh Water," in Repetto, ed., *The Global Possible*.

groundwater recharge and storing some of the summer floodwaters underground for the dry season. Much more work needs to be done on methods for recharging aquifers and managing groundwater and surface water resources conjunctively. Many of the obstacles are institutional. Throughout most of the world, groundwater is treated as an open-access, common-property resource, the water belongs to whoever "captures" it by pumping it to the surface. Unfortunately, anybody can degrade its quality with impunity by contaminating it with effluents. Subsurface water is becoming one of the most valuable of the world's common-property resources, but the losses from improper management are enormous. National and local governments urgently need to develop laws and institutions for managing and protecting these resources.

Protecting and managing watersheds is also crucial. In many parts of the world, deforestation and degradation of watersheds have reduced dry season river flows available for irrigation, exacerbated flooding in wet seasons, and diminished groundwater recharge. Erosion from deforested areas and poorly managed agricultural lands has increased siltation in watercourses and storage sites, shortening the useful lives of water projects.

Therefore, improving the management of upland farming and forest resources also pays off in better water resource management. India's Damodar Valley Corporation, a huge undertaking modeled after the Tennessee Valley Authority (TVA) in the United States to bring power, flood control, and irrigation to the three-hundred-mile-long valley of the Damodar, India's River of Sorrows, has promoted afforestation and erosion control throughout its thirty-year history. Its work reduced the rate of sedimentation from 1.34 to 0.08 hectare meters per year in the Panchet reservoir between 1956 and 1976, while raising average yields from rain-fed crops on the upland farms by 25 to 30 percent. Watershed protection programs that promote sound agro-forestry and water control practices in sensitive upland areas yield high returns in improved farm income and reduced environmental damages. Although national and international development agencies are directing more attention to these areas, current efforts are still small in comparison to needs and opportunities.

Planning water management projects must entail broad social

and environmental impact analysis and plans to mitigate effects on upland watersheds, on water-borne diseases, on waterlogging and salinization of soils, and on the socioeconomic structure of the communities affected. A widespread deficiency in the design of large irrigation projects has been failure to provide for any means to get the water back out after it has been brought in. The result has been the loss of millions of acres through gradual waterlogging and salinization. Where soils are poorly drained or water tables high, development agencies should require that drainage be installed when irrigation projects are constructed.

Since not all the consequences of projects that are often vast in scope can be anticipated, planning must become a continuous process that incorporates change. Provisions must be made to incorporate unexpected information, even after projects are completed. Whatever water management project is proposed, the people it will serve should participate in its planning and execution. Their knowledge of local conditions and of the operation of the system are essential to any project's success. International assistance organizations should insist that such processes be adopted before committing funds for project construction and should provide technical assistance to develop the capabilities of executing agencies.

The critical steps for controlling urban water pollution were discussed in the preceding section. These are essential in preserving water quality, but relying on "end-of-pipe" waste treatment is a costly mistake. Designing production systems for closed, circular flows of materials is usually the cheapest and most effective way of reducing pollution in the long run. Metals, oils, and other organic materials can be recovered and used productively. In-plant processes and balanced multiplant complexes that minimize wastes can be encouraged by appropriate incentives and planning. Recycling and reuse of water and materials and confined treatment and disposal of toxic and hazardous industrial wastes will enable developing countries to avoid the high costs and losses of environmental quality that many developed countries now face. Fiscal systems, environmental regulations, and public investments should be structured to encourage resource recovery as the primary approach to pollution control.

In rural areas, water quality is widely endangered by the runoff of fertilizers, pesticides, and highly mineralized irrigation water from farms. In many countries, subsidies to sales of pesticides and fertilizers, as well as to irrigation water, encourage excessive use. These subsidies could often be better devoted to research and extension programs on ecologically sound and agronomically effective farming systems.

Although the saying attributed to W. H. Auden that "few have died from lack of love, many have died from lack of water" is true, treating water uses as special needs rather than as economic demands impedes planning for wise use of the resource. Because water has been treated as a free good, people have come to expect to be able to take (and waste) as much as they want. Projecting these "needs" into the future creates the appearance of severe conflicts with resource availability. In fact, with efficient use and rational management, water need not constrain human progress.

AGRICULTURAL LAND

Doubling of world population and growth in per capita incomes will triple world food demands by the middle of the next century, according to the FAO. The prospects for meeting agricultural demands through the end of this century are excellent,[8] but whether the earth can support a tripling of food production is a debated question. The most optimistic assessments assert that as many as forty billion people could be fed—more than will ever inhabit the planet; the least optimistic put the figure closer to seven billion people—fewer than most reasonable projections say are inevitable. Low estimates of food production potential may underrate the rapid technological changes now occurring in agriculture and likely to result from the application of research findings in bioengineering. High estimates may understate the competing demands for land for nonagricultural uses and may overstate the ability of today's grasslands and tropical forests to support future crop production. They also assume intensive use of chemicals, water, and soils, which may not prove sustainable over the medium or long

8. FAO, *Agriculture: Toward 2000* (Rome: FAO, 1981).

term without modification of current farming methods. Although FAO studies predict that adequate land will be available for food production beyond the year 2000, other studies are far less optimistic, but the lack of detailed information on current land uses, land capabilities, and demand for land for nonagricultural uses makes it difficult to resolve the disagreements.

Much land currently in agricultural use is deteriorating because of inappropriate land and water management practices. One of the most comprehensive studies now available estimates that between the years 1975 and 2000, fifty million hectares of medium- and low-quality cropland will have been lost to erosion, along with twenty-five million hectares of grasslands and forests.[9] This represents about 3 percent of the cropland expected to be in use at the end of the century. Loss of topsoil through soil erosion is the most widespread form of land degradation, but salinization and waterlogging in some irrigated areas, such as those of the Sahel, remove irrigated hectares from cultivation as fast as new irrigation potential is created.

Most experts will agree that these are problems but disagree about how serious they are. Comprehensive, long-term data on the extent and rate of soil degradation and loss are scarce. Without this information, it is impossible to assess the capacity of the land base to support future populations or to plan corrective programs. Even in developed countries where data are better, little is known about the impact of losses on productivity, which depends on the specific characteristics of the land and its uses. Some authors stridently warn of a farmland crisis in the United States and Canada; others conclude that present rates of erosion could be borne without serious loss of productivity well into the middle of the next century. Moreover, looking only at soil losses is like examining only one side of a profit-and-loss statement. The same study that estimated the loss of fifty million hectares of cropland to erosion by the year 2000 predicts a net increase worldwide of three hundred million hectares through land conversion. Many farmers are also improving the quality of their soils through lev-

9. FAO and International Institute for Applied Systems Analysis, *Potential Population Supporting Capacities* (Rome: FAO, 1983).

eling, drainage, irrigation, and careful management of soil structure and nutrients.

Efforts by governments and international organizations to increase agricultural output have favored the flatter, better-watered lands. Agricultural modernization has largely bypassed the marginal regions on desert fringes and hilly uplands. It is precisely in these marginal areas that erosion is most serious, but farmers in these areas have remained among the poorest and the least able to invest in soil conservation. Without alternative sources of income and access to better land or improved technologies, farmers will continue to erode fragile lands in order to survive. On parts of Java, poor farmers continue to plant cassava and corn on fifty-degree slopes subject to heavy rainfall, largely because they cannot afford not to, even though their land can be ruined within a few years.

Soil erosion involves heavy off-farm costs too, such as downstream siltation and flooding. Where data are available, marked increases in sedimentation rates are observable, drastically shortening the lives of reservoirs and clogging watercourses. In West Java, rates have risen threefold in the past fifty years and sixfold in the past seventy-five years. Upland farmers have little time for concern about these downstream damages and, furthermore, can do little to correct the problem without active government involvement. Successful erosion control programs require the introduction of different farming systems, including the inputs and credit that farmers need to adopt them and the planning and implementation of reforestation and water control works on an area-wide basis.

Although many of the economic benefits of soil conservation are difficult to quantify, efforts to put dollar values on reduced soil fertility losses, improved water quality, reduced siltation of reservoirs and irrigation channels, and improved fish and wildlife habitat show that the benefits are significant. Moreover, improved farming systems that curtail erosion can also increase farm income severalfold by such changes as using high-productivity fodder shrubs and grasses to support stall-fed animals, by intercropping soil-stabilizing commercial trees with high-yielding annual crops, and by making additional inputs accessible to neglected farmers. The World Bank has found that many of its watershed protection projects, developed primarily to halt soil erosion in critical areas, offer extremely attractive economic rates of return. Here again, attending to basics can provide both environmental and economic benefits.

Many definitions of *sustainable agriculture* have been advanced, but a sensible perspective that includes the needs of present and future populations would include at least four considerations. First, production and productivity must continue to grow rapidly to meet rising demands. Second, agricultural practices must be nondestructive, so that the chemical nutrients removed by crops are replenished and the physical condition of the soil is maintained, acidity and toxic elements do not build up, erosion is controlled, and pests and diseases do not proliferate. Third, some form of land-use management must provide for competing land uses and reconcile the strong externalities that some land uses have on others. And fourth, continuing high levels of agricultural research must improve the technologies suitable for all current and potential agricultural zones, as defined by climatic, geological, ecological, and economic conditions.

Moving rapidly in this direction requires local participation in agricultural development programs to ensure that the people affected support them. This is likely only if such programs are compatible with local priorities and capabilities, do not undermine local institutions, and leave authority to the local community whenever possible. This support is absolutely essential for success. Billions of dollars have been spent on technically plausible development projects that failed because the people they were supposed to help did not want them. Agricultural development practitioners can tell stories of villagers who planted the trees provided for reforestation upside down, because they needed the land for more productive purposes, and of villages who would turn out at night with spades to dismantle the flood control works other laborers built by day, because they needed the water and its silt load for their fields.

Since most of the land with good agricultural potential is already being farmed, raising yields on these lands offers the best opportunity for increasing output, rather than bringing poorer lands into cultivation at ever higher costs. If better soils were used up to their yield potential, pressure on marginal lands would subside. In most developing countries, current yields of major crops are only one-third to one-half what they reasonably could be if existing technologies were successfully applied, and these yield frontiers continue to expand. It is worth remembering that in the agriculturally advanced countries, the cultivated area is generally smaller than it was at the beginning of the century, not because land has been lost but because it is no longer needed for crop production or is not economical to farm.[10]

By now, the pathways to sustainable growth in agricultural production are well known, if not well trodden. There are enough successful examples to demonstrate what could happen if all countries followed in the footsteps of the leaders. Even in low-income Asia and subsaharan Africa, where most of the world's hungry exist, some countries have achieved impressive gains in food production and availability.

The first step is pricing reform, and recognizing the productive potential of small-scale peasant agriculture. Throughout the developing world, agricultural prices have been manipulated to benefit the urban consumer and to provide resources for industrial development, at the expense of the poor farmer. In many countries, small farmers have been neglected; in some, they have been forced into cooperatives and collectives, usually with disastrous results. Eliminating macroeconomic and pricing policies that turn the internal terms of trade against farmers and undermine their incentives to produce is the first step toward sustainable agricultural development. If small farmers are provided with access to the technology and inputs to take advantage of more favorable incentives, they usually respond vigorously. In China, in the six years since agricultural policies were reversed to return responsibility for farm decisions to individual farmers and to allow agricultural prices to reflect market scarcities more accurately, farmers have responded by raising the value of agricultural output by 7 percent

10. Janos P. Hrabovszky, "Agriculture: The Land Base," in Repetto, ed., *The Global Possible*.

per year in real terms, even though land was scarce and yields were high to start with.

Raising farm prices is not enough, of course. Improving marketing, storage, and input distribution and credit systems is also necessary, if small farmers are to progress rapidly. So is strengthening agricultural extension methods, such as the training and visit system, that forge links between farmers and researchers. Zimbabwe provides a good example on the African continent, where agricultural success is hard to find. While preserving its large-scale commercial farms, the government has also attended to the needs of small farmers, providing access to credit and extension services. Zimbabwe has the best agricultural research system in Africa, and it works on subsistence and commercial crops alike. The government created grain depots in peasant farming areas and distribution centers for seeds, fertilizers, and tools. The consequence, despite setbacks from drought, has been a surplus of corn production from small farms and an overall trade surplus in agriculture.

No less than in industry, promoting sustainable production technologies in agriculture requires abandoning linear designs and emulating the complex networks of interaction found in nature. These farming systems rely on balance among organisms to control pest damages and maintain soil structure and fertility, thereby reducing both external inputs of energy and chemicals and discharges of wastes and effluents. A balanced approach to pest management that takes advantage of natural predation is one example. In Kwantung province in South China, rice farmers keep ducks in the rice paddies for weed and pest control and for extra income. Instead of heavy pesticide applications, these farmers plant varieties resistant to fungal disease, flood the paddies to destroy the larvae of rice borers, and release *Trichogramma* (tiny wasps whose eggs are deposited and mature in insect larvae) for additional pest control. They have been able to reduce their use of chemical pesticides and the associated costs by two-thirds.

There are several examples of tropical agricultural systems, such as the *pekarangan* of the Javanese or the milpas of Chiapan Mexicans, that use a dense mix of many diverse plant species to provide continuous ground cover against erosion and nutrient leaching, to recycle nutrients and capture all solar energy, and to reduce vulnerability to pest attacks.[11] Descendants of the Mayans plant more than 50 species of root, ground, and tree crops in their milpas; the Javanese plant as many as 150 species in their home gardens. These complex gardens are highly productive, keep the soil from depletion and erosion, and need no chemicals to keep pests under control. Agronomists are applying these principles to conventional farming systems with increasing success. Intercropping of grains with trees like the acacia that reduce wind erosion, keep the soil from drying out, and fix nitrogen in the root zone has raised yields on peasant farms by as much as 50 percent in several Sahelian countries. The unrealized potential of such diverse farming systems is large, especially in tropical areas, where temperate zone monocultures usually fail.

The first priority in reducing losses of agricultural lands should be to stem erosion and degradation where losses are now most severe. In the United States, for example, just 6 percent of the land growing crops contributed 43 percent of the soil lost to sheet and rill erosion. Ironically, these lands are typically not managed with conservation tillage and other erosion control programs. Soil conservation programs would be much more effective if targeted on critical areas and not undermined by broader agricultural policies that encourage farmers to plow up highly erodible lands— often to produce crops that are in surplus supply.[12]

In many countries, this will require a reversal of policies that have neglected marginal lands and marginal farmers. The best one-third of the world's cropland produces roughly two-thirds of the world's crops and is generally not subject to the most serious erosion losses. In Africa, however, the picture is quite different:

11. Otto Soemarwoto et al., "The Javanese Home Garden as an Integrated Ecosystem," *Science for Better Environment,* Proceedings of the International Congress on the Human Environment (Kyoto: 1975); James Nations and Ronald Nigh, "The Evolutionary Potential of Lacandon Maya Sustained-Yield Tropical Forest Agriculture," *Journal of Anthropological Research,* 36, no. 1 (Spring 1980): 1–31.

12. American Farmland Trust, *Soil Conservation in America* (Washington, D.C.: American Farmland Trust, 1984).

two-thirds of crop production comes from intermediate and inferior soils much more vulnerable to degradation. A major commitment of human and financial resources to less productive agricultural lands of the arid and semiarid tropics, tropical moist forest regions, and hilly uplands is required.

Soil erosion and land degradation must be controlled from both inside and outside the agricultural sector. In Indonesia, where more than a million hectares are seriously eroding in the uplands of Java, part of any solution must be measures to provide more jobs in rural areas and towns, so that poor households now desperately trying to grow cassava and corn on slopes as steep as fifty degrees can find other ways to survive. The same could be said of Nepal, El Salvador, and other countries where highly marginal lands are used for subsistence farming by impoverished peasants with few alternatives. Slower population growth and opportunities to migrate and work elsewhere are essential.

Nevertheless, much can also be accomplished within the agricultural sector. In the United States, for example, agricultural price supports, low-interest loans, tax write-offs for land development, and other provisions have contributed to the expansion of cultivation onto vulnerable grazing lands and wetlands, while land set-aside programs have not removed the most erodible lands from cultivation.

In the developing countries, the key is increasing agricultural extension services to promote appropriate farming systems in vulnerable areas, such as interplanting high-yielding forage, food, and tree crops, conservation tillage and mulching, and terracing for water control. These improved systems will be adopted rapidly only if profitable and if credit, inputs, and marketing facilities are available to small farmers. Usually, marginal lands and marginal farmers get only marginal attention from agricultural development agencies.

In many countries, the concentration of landholdings adds to the pressures on fragile and marginal lands. In Peru, Honduras, and El Salvador, for example, where the uplands are deteriorating, the one-half of all farmers who have the smallest holdings control in total less than 5 percent of all the agricultural land. Large estates, which are often on flatter and richer soils, tend to be used less intensively than eroding hillside plots. This is one of the many reasons why agrarian reform should be high on the priority list of measures to improve resource management.

Land-use planning and management have been impeded by the lack of data on land capabilities, uses, and vulnerability to degradation. Currently, efforts are under way to improve the data base. Satellite photographic imagery can produce soil and land-use maps on more detailed scales than those currently available worldwide, and data overlays incorporating topography, basal geology, temperature, and rainfall can show an area's erosion potential. Rapidly improving technology can make relatively modest investments in systematic data collection highly worthwhile, provided the results are closely linked to the planning process and land-use planning is enforced through zoning and other controls and actually guides major investment decisions.

Research into soil conservation and sustainable agriculture also requires increased support. International research centers should establish closer linkages with national research institutions and pay more explicit attention to dissemination. In developing countries, research institutions generally need improved training of scientists and managers, better physical facilities, and closer contacts with extension services at home and other research institutions abroad. Among the many topics in need of research attention are the technical, economic, and social considerations in better soil management. Other specific research priorities to improve the sustainability of agriculture include development of drought and disease-resistant crop varieties, pest control strategies that balance use of chemical inputs with use of other means of pest control, more efficient irrigation practices, and high-productivity mixed-cropping and animal husbandry systems.

By pursuing these strategies, global land resources can be preserved and adequate food production ensured for future generations. Much can be done to continually increase agricultural production, and the essential changes needed to conserve the land base are neither very large nor very difficult to achieve.

TROPICAL FORESTS

Although forests in the developed world are holding their own, despite threats from air pollution, the area of forests in the developing countries has declined by half since 1900 and is shrinking by about eleven million hectares each year, mainly because of increasing farmlands. The accelerating loss of tropical forest cover has immediate and long-range socioeconomic and ecological consequences.

Some 150 million hectares of tropical watersheds, most of them seriously degraded, are threatened by over-grazing and soil erosion. Among the consequences are increased flooding, sedimentation of dams and reservoirs, disruption of downstream irrigation systems, and losses of crops, land—and even human life.

A significant proportion of the millions of species sheltered by tropical forests, the most biologically diverse ecosystems on earth, will become extinct by the end of this century, as a further one hundred million hectares of forest disappear.

Fuelwood scarcities in some fifty-seven developing countries affect more than one billion people. Among other adverse repercussions, this scarcity forces farmers to burn about four hundred million tons of animal dung a year. If this dung were instead used to improve soil fertility, grain production could be about twenty million tons a year more.

As a result of past overcutting and inadequate investment in forest management and new plantations, twenty developing countries that have climates and land resources well suited to industrial forestry now import manufactured forest products, valued in excess of $50 million a year. In another fourteen countries that depend heavily on foreign exchange derived from tropical hardwood exports, the more valuable species are being "mined" and will soon run out.[13]

The underlying reasons for deforestation in the tropics include inequalities in land tenure; rural poverty; the pressure of expanding populations; relatively low agricultural productivity; underinvestment in forestry; the general ineffectiveness of state and national forestry agencies; and the lack of integrated planning among forestry, agriculture, energy, health, and other sectors. They will not yield to halfhearted efforts to halt the process. Yet forests can make a much larger sustained contribution to economic de-

13. John Spears and Edward S. Ayensu, "Resources, Development, and the New Century: Forestry," in Repetto, ed., *The Global Possible*.

velopment, particularly to agricultural productivity and the welfare of the rural poor. Deforestation must be controlled in order to maintain the essential ecological processes and life-support systems on which human survival and well-being depend, to preserve genetic diversity, and to help ensure the continuing availability of resources that support millions of rural communities and major industries.

There is not one forestry problem in the tropics, but several. International efforts need to be directed toward (a) rehabilitating and protecting upland watersheds; (b) protecting the world's fast-shrinking, biologically diverse tropical rain forests; (c) solving the fuelwood crisis; (d) reducing developing-country dependence on forest product imports and ensuring sustained tropical timber exports; and (e) developing the institutional capacity within the developing countries to support stronger integrated management and conservation of tropical forest resources on a sustainable basis.

The general lack of recognition of tropical deforestation as a priority concern by national and international development agencies and woefully inadequate levels of past investment have been largely responsible for the alarming forestry situation that prevails today in most developing countries. Improved forest management must become an integral part of rural development and regional land-use planning.

Many of the socioeconomic and technical measures to reduce tropical deforestation are already known. Given increased political commitment and resources, it will be possible to contain deforestation in many developing countries before the turn of the century. What is needed is a concerted international effort to implement an action plan that identifies priority areas for investment in forestry and related sectors and corrects misguided policies.

Foresters alone cannot solve these problems. Raising agricultural productivity and rural incomes through the initiatives discussed above will provide people with alternatives to forest encroachment. In some countries, land reforms that open up broader access to farmland to the rural poor are vital, if the destruction of forests is to stop. This could, in the short term, do more to relieve pressure on forest lands than any other single policy intervention or any realistic level of investment in forest resource development, but it requires strong political commitment by governments and the support of development agencies.

Given the current rate of tropical forest loss, greater resources must be directed to managing and conserving the remaining forest areas. Few countries have set aside enough forested area to ensure the preservation of disappearing species and ecosystems, and areas marked for protection or conservation are often inadequately managed. In the long term, a substantially increased investment in research to overcome the existing paucity of knowledge of tropical forest ecosystems is required.

Rehabilitation of Degraded Watersheds

The most effective long-run method of restoring watersheds is to reduce the number of people living in them. Once population pressure is lifted, the poorer mountainous areas can be maintained through sustainable agriculture. This will occur when economic development raises the productivity of land and provides more job opportunities in lowland areas.

However, the chances of reducing population pressures on forests, soils, and water resources in the short run are just about nil in most developing countries. The only practical way to proceed is to provide farmers and communities in these watersheds with the necessary inputs and technical support systems they need to improve farm productivity and to minimize erosion and flooding. In upland watersheds, control of forest grazing and logging needs special attention, as does promoting higher-productivity mixed agro-forestry and husbandry farming systems, increasing soil conservation and flood control works, and ensuring adequate farm credit and price incentives.

Programs to rehabilitate degraded watersheds are planned and carried out much more effectively if governments recognize watersheds as discrete planning units. India is implementing integrated rural development projects on thirty-one critical watersheds—for example, incorporating agriculture, horticulture, animal husbandry, forestry, water resource development, and other components across each basin as a project unit. The Indian experience has demonstrated how interrelated all these activities are and how upstream activities affect the success of downstream programs. It also illustrates the important role local private voluntary organizations and community associations can—and must—play. The Chipko Movement, for example, effectively agitated for forest preservation and has organized successful tree plantations.

Community movements have been successful in Korea in reforesting more than three hundred thousand hectares of upland forests, mostly on privately owned land in eleven thousand villages. Owners contract with village forestry associations for reforestation and management in return for 10 percent of the output. This success has been possible within a strongly disciplined community development program directed by the central government.

In central China, where the watershed of the Yellow River discharges several billion tons of loess sediment each year and aggravates flooding in the densely populated lowlands, community associations have made remarkable progress in rehabilitation. Of the 868 square kilometers of severely eroded land in Chunhua County, 42 percent has been restored in five years by terracing with hand labor and replanting with fruit orchards and poplar windbreaks. Fifteen million trees have been planted, one hundred per resident of the county, and sediment transport has been cut in half.

Preservation of Threatened Forest Ecosystems

Establishing a comprehensive network of protected biological reserves requires setting aside at least a hundred million hectares of threatened tropical forests (10 percent of the remaining area). It is useless to hope that the countries in the developing world with most of the tropical forests and exceptional biological endowments will do this without the assistance of the rest of the world. Biological resources are global common property, and a cooperative framework for their management must be evolved. The developed countries with the scientific and industrial capability to profit from these genetic endowments cannot act like "free riders" but will have to share in the costs, if an expansion in protected areas of this order of magnitude is to be achieved.

The first step is to identify crisis situations, where whole eco-systems are on the verge of disappearing. Madagascar, for example, is a world museum of evolution, isolated from mainland Africa for a hundred million years. It has an exceptionally large number of species found nowhere else: 80 percent of the ten thousand plant species are endemic; five families and thirty-four genera of mammals, including lemurs and other primates; four families and thirty-six genera of birds. Eighty percent of the island's forests have been cleared, and the remaining area under tropical forest, mostly along the eastern coast, will be destroyed by slash-and-burn agriculture and logging by the end of the century unless drastic action is taken. Existing conservation areas must be more strictly protected, others must be created—including new types that are managed effectively for multiple uses, and conservation objectives must be incorporated into national development plans.

Although there are many such crises, a longer-term strategy must still be developed, and there is a useful role for aid agencies and nongovernmental conservation agencies like the International Union for the Conservation of Nature (IUCN), the World Wildlife Fund, and others. For one thing, they can help the twenty-six priority developing countries identified by the IUCN's Commission on National Parks and Protected Areas carry out systematic ecological surveys aimed at identifying biologically unique areas of tropical forests that should be conserved.

Aid agencies have been reluctant to help finance conservation activities, perhaps because of the mistaken notion that they are not productive investments. However, the direct economic benefits that flow from genetic resources found in the wild have been amply documented,[14] and aid agencies could directly fund conservation-oriented projects in developing countries as long-run investments. More can also be done to ensure that good planning, mitigation activities, and compensatory set-asides minimize adverse effects of development projects on tropical forest ecosystems.

Highways, dams, and other large-scale developments fre-

14. Norman Myers, *The Primary Source* (New York: W. W. Norton, 1984); Margery Oldfield, *The Value of Conserving Genetic Resources* (Washington, D.C.: U.S. Department of the Interior, National Park Service, 1984).

quently open up areas with rich biological resources to highly disruptive activities that are not adequately controlled. Land settlement projects can instead be channelled into nonforest lands, especially those areas where land can be reclaimed (such as the *ylang-ylang* grassland areas in Indonesia and the Philippines). Rural development programs should create buffer zones along the forest fringe by intensifying agricultural productivity, introducing land reform and employment programs, and providing social services to enable these populations to settle in more permanent communities. Where suitable soils lie beneath forest lands, forest-dwelling families will adopt proven agro-forestry farming systems, based on greater use of agricultural tree crops. In Indonesia, for example, the government has established a new policy in its large-scale transmigration program that resettles Javanese on the outer islands: virtually all new settlers will be put on agro-forestry projects and rely mainly on tree crops for income.

As they will benefit from the preservation of tropical forests, and because most developing countries have insufficient resources, developed country governments must assume a significant proportion of the costs required to establish an effective network of conservation areas. The United States and other developed countries should take the lead in creating an International Conservation Fund to subsidize the establishment of protected areas in tropical forests and to increase support for the World Heritage Parks and Man and the Biosphere Programs.

Fuelwood and Multipurpose Tree Planting

In many developing countries, rural people rely on wood for 80 percent or more of their cooking fuel, and consumption exceeds the annual sustainable supply by huge margins: by 70 percent in the Sudan, 150 percent in Ethiopia, and 800 percent in Mauritania. Deforestation accelerates as demands grow with increasing populations and stocks decrease; then wind erosion, desiccation of soils, and loss of ground cover and of nutrients follow as local people turn increasingly to crop residues for fuel and fodder. In some countries, a quickening downward spiral is already evident.[15]

This comes close to being a true tragedy of the commons. Deforestation is occurring overwhelmingly on public lands that are inadequately managed or on which villagers have traditional cutting rights. Trees are destroyed instead of being coppiced or pollarded for higher sustained yields, and reforestation efforts that are too small to begin with often fail from inadequate care, excessive grazing, fires, or overcutting. The sad irony is that this exploitation of public lands also cripples private initiative by keeping fuelwood prices so low despite the scarcity that, except in the vicinity of some cities, private entrepreneurs cannot earn an adequate return on fuelwood plantations that must be tended for several years before harvest.

Solving this institutional problem is the key. Ample experience shows that farmers will jump to plant trees when the returns are high. Profits are available from plantations that yield poles, fruit, fodder, or other products in addition to fuelwood, and striking successes have been observed in as wide a range of countries as India, Haiti, and China. In the Indian state of Gujarat, many farmers have shifted from growing cotton to eucalyptus, which offers a rate of return on costs in excess of 100 percent and reduces peak labor demands. From 12 million trees in 1975, the yearly planting rate has grown to 100 million in 1981 and 195 million in 1983. Although not the main product, almost one-third of the harvest— mostly tops and thinnings—is available for fuelwood. The Gujarat government initiated the program with subsidized seedlings and buy-back agreements with tree nurseries established by schools and private farmers. Now tree farming in Gujarat has tremendous momentum of its own.

In China, as part of the return of farming to private responsibility, individuals can now contract for the use of waste lands for tree plantations. The response has been vigorous, and more than eight million farmers are already taking part. Some are profiting

15. Dennis Anderson and Robert Fishwick, *Fuelwood Consumption and Deforestation in Africa*, Staff Working Paper no. 704 (Washington, D.C.: World Bank, 1985).

handsomely from their initiative in planting nurseries and high-value tree crops.

This is one solution to the problems of the commons: transfer them to private management along with the risks and rewards from their use. This approach has usually been more successful than attempts to promote village woodlots or to stop illicit exploitation of public forests, except where strong traditions of community organization still thrive. In West Bengal, for example, experience with community woodlots has been disappointing, but a program that gives landless peasants title to small plots of government wasteland for tree planting has done well. In Tanzania as well, communal efforts have faltered, but farmers carefully fence, water, and fertilize their private seedlings—and a much higher percentage survives.

If the fivefold increase in planting needed to approach a balance of demand and sustainable supply in rural areas of the developing world is to be achieved, much greater effort must go into developing—and backstopping—programs that involve communities and private producers. Fast-growing, high-yielding, soil-restoring multipurpose tree species are recognized, but more research is needed on improved varieties and species attractive to local communities, and the availability of tree nurseries must grow rapidly. Acknowledged planting and management techniques can greatly raise the sustainable yield, but these need to be explained and demonstrated to farmers. Forestry agencies that have worked with commercial timber companies or tried to act as policemen must become involved with peasants and villages to promote small-scale developments.

Industrial Forestry

Although natural resources are being depleted rapidly in the best-endowed countries, the scope for increased productivity and production of industrial forest products is enormous, especially in tropical countries in South America, Central Africa, and Southeast Asia, with large, sparsely populated areas suitable for forestry. In these countries today, most timber comes from selective felling of high-value tree species from almost unmanaged forests. In Malaysia, the Philippines, the Ivory Coast, Indonesia, and other major producing countries, these stocks are being exhausted. Yields per acre are only a small fraction of those from intensively managed closed forests in Europe and North America, and these yields decline over time as less valuable species take over the regrowth or accessible logged-over areas are converted to farming or ranching. Outside India, where colonial forest management traditions have been maintained, less than 2 percent of closed forests in the developing world are intensively managed for sustained timber production. Industrial plantations, which offer sustained yields many times higher than lightly managed natural forests, also account for no more than 2 percent of the total closed forest area. Expanding the area under plantations and managing natural closed forests better can not only allow developing countries to meet the rapid growth in their own demands for forest products, but can also allow them to compete successfully for the largely stable demand of the industrial world. But more applied research into the techniques and economics of sustained yield management of these natural forests is needed.

Success in well-endowed countries will depend largely on governments' political commitment. More muscle has to back up stipulations in timber contracts with concessionaires covering less wasteful logging, fuller use of species and wood by-products, and regeneration programs. Many of the forestry agencies that oversee concessions have severe management problems and cave in under the heavy pressures they face.

Since the productivity of extensively managed natural tropical forests is relatively low and the natural forests remaining in many countries are too small to supply domestic market needs, increasing emphasis should be placed on short-rotation industrial plantations of fast-growing commercial species on already deforested lands. The economic and financial returns are relatively favorable, the land requirements much less, and the risks to remaining natural forests are greatly reduced. Only about 10 percent of the cutover area of productive forests could meet all the demands of developing countries for industrial products in the year 2000.

The industrial private sector can be encouraged to accelerate the pace of investment in industrial plantations. Chile's policy of granting rather generous tax incentives doubled the rate of planting and virtually replaced public with private activity. By the end of 1983, more than a million hectares of plantations were established, and forest-based exports exceeded $350 million per year. With a stable economic and policy environment that facilitates long-term planning, it is likely that substantial business investment will take place in many countries without appreciable subsidies, given the production potential and rapidly expanding markets.

Forestry Research, Education, and Training

Sustained support of an international program in tropical forestry research, education, and training is essential to the overall success of the initiatives outlined here. The weakness of forestry services in many countries makes the implementation of forest management or conservation plans totally impossible, and the scientific basis for management of tropical forests is weak or totally absent. According to Dr. S. H. Sohmer of the National Science Foundation, "We should never lose sight of the fact that we know little or nothing about the way humid tropical forests are structured and how they evolve." Further, even the most basic data are often missing. When Thailand completed a forest inventory based on remote sensing data, the government found that only 25 percent of its land area was forested, not 48 percent as it had been assuming.

The emphasis in tropical forestry research should be shifted toward the sociological aspects of forestry; basic scientific research aimed at increasing the biological productivity of agro-forestry systems, fuelwood, and multipurpose trees for use in rural areas; conservation (particularly in the areas of energy consumption and preserving biological diversity); and sustained research into national forest-management systems. Developed and developing country governments, universities, the industrial private sector, international research centers, and multilateral aid agencies all have significant roles to play.

The main challenge that currently confronts almost all developing countries is restructuring traditional forest services, most of which have been primarily concerned with policing government-owned forest reserves. Education and training will play a key role in reorienting the mission of forest services to providing technical extension support for the thousands of small farmers, village communities, private companies, and nongovernmental organizations that will be actors in the main rural reforestation programs.

If an action program designed to tackle these forestry problems is implemented worldwide, the benefits could include restoration of 150 million hectares of degraded watersheds; increased food production and farm income for thirty million families already residing in watersheds; reduced downstream flooding and more stable agriculture for up to five hundred million people; assured domestic fuelwood supplies for one billion families; preservation of 100 million hectares of tropical forest and hundreds of thousands of plant and animal species that would otherwise be extinct; improved and sustainable farm income for twenty million forest-dwelling families; and, additional foreign exchange savings or earnings of $10 billion a year.

BIOLOGICAL DIVERSITY

Although the ultimate fate of practically all species is extinction, humans have become earth's executioners. Definitive data are scarce, but the rate at which species are disappearing seems to have risen four hundred times above the long-run historical average. We can reasonably assume that a species a day is dying out and that this rate will increase during the coming decades unless action is taken. The California condor is on the brink of disappearing from the mountains. Siberian cranes, orangutans, and many others are equally endangered. The background extinction rate for *families* of species has been about two to five extinctions per *million* years; yet in the next century, one-quarter of all plant families (more than fifty) may disappear, along with their many associated insect and other animal families. Scientists estimate that 20 percent or more of all the species on earth will die out within the next generation. If this happens, more than one million species of animals and plants will be gone forever.[16]

The damages to humankind are truly inestimable, because most of these species will disappear before humans have learned anything about their potential uses. As the explosive growth of the science of genetic engineering continues and as pressures on agricultural and natural systems increase, genetic variability will be increasingly valuable.This places a premium on maintaining a broad array of genetic reservoirs in the wild. In agriculture, wild strains of rice contributed notably to the seed improvements that drove the Green Revolution, and all the major cereal crops depend on inputs of wild genes for continued resistance to pests and diseases. The $3 billion in foreign exchange earnings from Latin America's coffee crop was saved from ruinous rust disease in 1970 when a rust-resistant strain was found in the forests of Ethiopia. It is estimated that prospective breakthroughs in genetic engineering will generate products worth $50 to $100 billion a year before the end of the century. Major contributions are to be expected in the industrial and medical sectors as well. The genes in wild species are solutions to biological problems that have evolved over millions of years. Their loss is irreversible.

Threats to biological diversity are found throughout the world, but the most urgent are in the tropics, where 40 percent of the earth's species are found. The primary danger is the destruction of habitats (both terrestrial and marine), as ever growing human populations seek the means for survival. The Atlantic forest of eastern Brazil is home to the last two hundred of the spectacular golden lion tamarin. Although the forest was nearly pristine 150 years ago, less than 1 percent now remains in scattered and dwindling fragments as agricultural and commercial conversions grow. Since people's aspirations to a decent life come first, long-run success in conserving biological diversity depends, first and foremost, on finding ways to meet these human needs without excessive habitat destruction.

National governments, scientific institutes, and international

16. Kenton R. Miller *et al.*, "Issues on the Preservation of Biological Diversity," in Repetto, ed., *The Global Possible*.

voluntary agencies have provided a solid foundation for future conservation efforts. Gene banks, tissue and organ collections, botanical gardens and zoos, and game farms and ranches pursue *ex situ* preservation. More than 3000 protected sites covering in excess of 450,000,000 hectares in at least 120 countries preserve habitats in the majority of the world's biogeographic regions. A worldwide network of institutions published in 1980 the *World Conservation Strategy,* a framework for conserving biological diversity while achieving sustainable development.

Yet the quiet crisis continues. Despite occasional uproars over snail darters and pandas, the disappearance of species is usually silent and unnoticed. The importance of the problem has not caught the public's attention either in developed or in developing countries, nor has it elicited strong action by the world's governments. Measures to conserve natural habitats, the most important actions governments can take, are often viewed as impediments to development.

Humankind has always considered nature's abundance a free gift—free for the taking. Institutions and attitudes reflect that. Wild creatures are usually considered available to all in the community before they are captured. The wilderness must be tamed and "improved" before it can be legally possessed. Although horses can be owned, the idea that the genetic material pooled in the horse species can be subject to property rights still seems strange.

These arrangements are anachronistic, now that the human species has expanded to crowd out many others. Property rights have evolved to encourage the care and effective use of resources, but biological resources lack this—or equivalent—protection. The common-property aspect of biological diversity contributes to the inability of societies to value and conserve this resource effectively. Actions to conserve biological diversity are hampered by a "free rider" problem of global scale: no way has been found to assess individuals or societies around the world for the benefits they derive from conservation efforts, and most beneficiaries are content to let others carry the burden.

Without the relevant facts at their disposal and without a corresponding awareness in the audiences they address, even sympathetic policymakers find it hard to press the case for conservation. Neither governments nor citizens are aware of the value of biological diversity or the real threats to it. Even such fundamentals as its links to agriculture, industry, energy, and health need to be more widely understood. Eighty percent of prescription drugs for hypotension in the 1960s were derived from rauwolfia, a traditional Indian remedy for nervous disorders and dysentery. A species of Mexican yam yields diosgenin, the source of 95 percent of steroid drugs on the market today. The rosy periwinkle, a small West Indian flower, gives lymphocytic leukemia patients a 99-percent chance of recovery and has dramatically improved treatment of Hodgkin's disease. Despite these successes, scientific knowledge of most species and their ecosystems is too scanty to permit adequate conservation or use of these resources, and it must be expanded.

Although substantial investments in land, finance, and institutional support to protect important biomes have been made, current management of these areas often does not provide effective protection. Garamba National Park in Zaire contains the last viable natural population of the endangered northern white rhino, but their numbers have fallen from 259 in 1975 to 15 or 20 individuals today because of professional poaching. Some critical unprotected habitats are also rapidly disappearing. In Ecuador, the coastal forest, which is said to have the world's greatest plant diversity—six hundred species per square kilometer—has been almost completely replaced by banana and oil palm plantations. Also, the mangrove forests of Ecuador, along with those of most other countries, are quickly being cut down and filled for other coastal developments, and the critical breeding grounds and habitats they provide are being lost. Thus, another key step is to design and implement immediate programs to avert impending wholesale losses in imperiled regions, along with longer-term programs to establish and maintain a network of parks and reserves that preserves each major biome.

Thirty-one countries have completed or are formulating national conservation strategies. Yet practical guidelines for maintaining biological diversity and integrating conservation and development plans are still in short supply. Other nations that draw up conservation strategies can learn from this experience and integrate their concern for biological resources more effectively into economic development planning and policymaking.

Many of the international conventions and treaties that were drawn up to increase international cooperation in conservation have foundered, because national governments have not given them adequate financial and policy support. The World Heritage Convention that provides support for World Heritage Parks of special ecological or cultural significance is grossly underfunded. The accomplishments of other agreements, such as the Western Hemisphere Convention, which could have provided for much more international cooperation in protecting and studying migratory bird species, have been disappointing. At the same time, inadequate private property rights prevent private efforts to utilize and conserve natural genetic resources. It is essential for the long run to develop institutions, international agreements, and economic incentives that express the value of biological resources and strengthen private and government efforts to conserve them.

Specific actions can be taken to resolve these problems. Perhaps the most easily manageable is broadening public interest and awareness. NGOs such as the Environmental Liaison Center, the IUCN, the World Wildlife Fund, and regional or local organizations can lead a worldwide publicity campaign to raise general consciousness of the value of biological diversity. Foundations and other bodies already dedicated to environmental conservation, such as the National Audubon Society, and environmental education centers around the world have the capacity to support it. A highlight of this campaign could be a major world event, staged to draw the attention of policymakers.

But increased efforts by national NGOs are also needed to bring these issues to the attention of national policymakers. To help in illuminating the shade in which most species go unrecognized and unappreciated, the business community, governments, and international institutions should expand financial support for research in tropical biology and related fields devoted to the discovery and investigation of genetic resources. Universities and other research bodies could expand cooperative programs with counterparts in countries with rich biological resources.

That so little such research is carried out or supported by industry at first seems paradoxical, in view of the commercial value of products derived from wild species. Natural pesticides abound that may not impose the risks to nontarget organisms many synthetics do. For example, rotenoids from the roots of forest-growing legumes in Amazonia and Southeast Asia make powerful sprays for field crops and dips for livestock. Forty-one percent of the prescription sales of pharmaceuticals in the United States contain a drug of natural origin. Yet little work to explore the possible beneficial uses of millions of unknown species of plants, insects, and animals is under way.[17] Global spending on tropical research is less than $40 million per year. Some five thousand kinds of fish live in the drainage basin of the Amazon River, as many as in the Atlantic Ocean, but almost half have never even been catalogued. The main impediment is that under current property rules in most countries, the value of naturally occurring organisms cannot be appropriated by private parties. It is another example of the common-property problem.

An urgent effort is required to protect critical endangered ecosystems, such as the remaining tropical forests of Madagascar. The IUCN should disseminate to key NGOs and international agencies its priority list of endangered habitats, so that they can consult with national governments in countries containing those areas to modify ongoing activities and put in place new programs to protect them. The NGO community has technical expertise and interim funding to contribute where it is needed to get this effort under way. Conservation efforts will be more successful in protecting all significant biomes if national efforts are coordinated. For example, regional working teams pulled together by the IUCN's Commission on National Parks and Protected Areas are identifying important gaps in international coverage.

New approaches are called for to establish additional protected areas that fill these gaps. The key problem is devising ways that developed countries, the main beneficiaries in the long run, can effectively support the conservation effort. The multilateral de-

17. Peter H. Raven, *Research Priorities in Tropical Biology* (Washington, D.C.: National Research Council, 1980).

velopment banks, for example, can include in their lending programs the projects and project components to establish and manage protected areas, develop buffer zones around them, and provide technical assistance and training to management agencies in borrowing countries. Where these projects are sited in upper watersheds, which need to be protected to preserve downstream water resource investments, or near highway developments that would lead to disruptive land settlements and population influxes without protective measures, such components are naturally complementary to the kinds of development loans multilateral banks now make. These projects can be framed to contribute to the economic development in the regions concerned, by expanding income-generating opportunities outside the protected areas and in buffer zones.

A good example of this approach is the Dumoga-Bone National Park on the island of Sulawesi in Indonesia. The three hundred thousand hectares of this primary forest reserve lie in the upper watershed of a large water storage and irrigation scheme that the World Bank helped finance. By preventing disturbance or destruction of the forest, the Park protects the reservoir from siltation and helps regulate water flow. The World Bank convinced itself that the investment to establish the park was worthwhile on these grounds alone and incorporated this component into its loan. But the Park also contains large populations of most of Sulawesi's endemic birds and mammals and serves as an important scientific field research station.

Management plans for existing conservation areas can be based on already developed and tested methods and experience on all continents. The Proceedings from the Bali Action Plan of the 1982 World Congress on National Parks contain 120 case histories of success. Successful plans provide for ample consultations with groups living in and near protected areas, preserve to the greatest extent possible customary usage and systems of resource management, and provide compensation and alternatives for local residents whose livelihoods are affected.

There is a universal shortage of trained personnel to carry out the tasks necessary for conserving biological diversity. Tropical foresters, geneticists, agronomists, conservation administrators, taxonomists, protected areas managers, and many other kinds of specialists are badly needed. Without them, the problem cannot be solved.

University programs need to be strengthened in fields such as genetics, taxonomy, resource management, administration, forestry, and ecology. The basic curricula have already been developed at the Missouri Botanical Gardens and the School of Natural Resources of the University of Michigan in the United States, New Zealand's Lincoln College, the College of African Wildlife Management in Tanzania, the Forestry Faculty at the National Agrarian University of Peru, and others.

Midlevel training programs should also be strengthened to prepare qualified field personnel, who are in short supply. Costa Rica and Venezuela, for example, both have progressive wildlife laws and parks programs but lack the personnel to enforce their regulations. Much can be gained by improving the management of existing conservation areas. The College of African Wildlife Management at Mweka, Tanzania, has trained more than a thousand game wardens and assistants, who now staff all of East Africa's conservation areas, direct training institutions in other African countries, and even run the conservation programs in several countries. This outstanding early example is a model for training programs that raise the competence and professional standing of wildlife management personnel.

Better management of national parks is by no means enough, however. Conservation objectives have to figure into sectoral and national economic plans and policies. Although the contribution of national park services and government agencies specifically responsible for the preservation of natural areas is essential, the lead role should be taken by the national agency with overall responsibility for economic planning and coordination, so that the resultant national conservation strategy will be an integral part of development plans and policy. For example, land capability surveys and land-use plans should include the value of areas as habitat and establish procedures to ensure that these classifications will be used in preinvestment planning. Development activities, such as road construction and land settlement projects, should generally be located away from undisturbed natural areas.

Bilateral and multilateral development agencies can help by improving their own assessment of project impacts on critical habitats and biological resources and can include mitigation and compensatory set-asides in projects when adverse impacts are identified. These agencies should also support applied research to improve ecological impact assessment and to quantify the benefits from preserving natural systems.

Stronger financial support for existing international instruments for ensuring conservation is needed. Even considered together, however, these instruments are inadequate to achieve biological diversity goals. A new, comprehensive international convention to help fund the network of representative protected areas would overcome the common-property problem. The benefits of conservation accrue to all countries, not just to those in which the resources are located. Such a convention would provide that countries requiring support would agree to protect the areas and would receive funds for management and other purposes from an international fund to which all nations would contribute.

At the national level, governments could accomplish a great deal by reviewing existing business tax codes, development incentives, public sector infrastructure investments, and policies governing the lease and use of public lands to ensure that timber, energy, agricultural, and ranching industries are not receiving subsidies and other benefits that encourage their encroachment into natural areas to a greater extent than would occur without such government support. Notorious examples of such policies that effectively promote habitat loss, such as Brazil's tax support for huge cattle ranches in the Amazon and Indonesia's massive transmigration program to the forests of the outer islands, are just indicators of a widespread bias against conservation in development policies.

Further investigations and policy analysis should be carried out to identify appropriate changes in tax codes and other incentives that encourage private enterprises, nonprofit organizations, and individuals to preserve natural habitats and contribute to conservation areas, including areas in foreign countries. Particular attention should be given to mechanisms that establish or extend property rights in genetic resources.

These initiatives to preserve a valuable natural resource must be regarded as investments in the human future, if they are to have any chance for adoption. Examples of the payoffs are compelling. A recently discovered form of wild corn, growing in its last four hectares of habitat in a Mexican forest, not only harbors perennial traits and tolerates soils too wet for conventional varieties but also shows immunity or tolerance to at least four of eight leading viruses and mycoplasmas that now destroy 1 percent of the world's corn harvest—a loss of more than $500 million. The irreversible loss of such genetic marvels can be prevented with manageable adjustments in policies and priorities.

ENERGY

The sixfold increase in the real price of oil since 1972, with its powerful repercussions on the world economy, brought the entire world to a sense of urgency about energy policy. Events have revealed how inextricably bound energy policy is to global economic growth and stability, poverty, environmental preservation, and political and military security. Responses to energy problems affect the attainment not just of a sustainable energy supply but also of a sustainable world.

Conventional energy strategies that anticipate future reliance mainly on coal and nuclear energy pay insufficient attention to six important factors. These include (a) the environmental impacts of expanded fossil fuel use, (b) the threat of nuclear weapons proliferation implicit in widespread nuclear fuel enrichment and reprocessing, (c) the political and economic vulnerability of economies highly dependent on imported energy, (d) the pressing energy needs of the rural sector in developing countries, (e) the economic impact of expanding energy use in the industrial countries on the growth of developing countries, and (f) the effects of energy scarcities and economic instability on the world's poor.

A soft oil market, partly due to worldwide recession from 1981 to 1983, has diverted attention from the central fact that sometime in the next twenty-five years or so, global oil production (not including natural gas) will very likely begin to decline. As a result, there will begin a gradual transition to an era in which oil no longer dominates global energy markets. This transition can be accomplished with minimal disruption through appropriate incentives, foresight and planning, investment, and research.

But it will not be easy. Long investment lead times; technological, environmental, and economic uncertainties; conflicting domestic interests; and international conflicts all stand in the way. By far the most promising means of satisfying new energy needs are energy conservation, the improvement of energy efficiency, and the development of renewable energy sources. In the industrial countries, the energy challenge is to pursue this strategy intensively enough to ensure adequate energy supplies without jeopardizing the broader aspects of sustainability detailed above.

In the developing countries, most people depend on noncommercial biomass fuels, especially for domestic uses. As the earlier section on forestry has described, shortages of fuelwood and other biomass sources have caused serious deforestation in many countries and the loss of vegetative and animal manures from the soil. Unless adequate and affordable supplies are available, problems of environmental degradation and poverty will increase. At the same time, industrialization and urbanization are proceeding rapidly in many developing countries. Those without indigenous energy resources have faced heavy oil import bills that have helped create the current international debt crisis. Again, improvements in energy efficiency and conservation, as well as accelerated efforts to expand the role of renewable energy sources, constitute a promising long-run strategy.

The basic physical laws of conservation of energy and matter imply that the massive conversion of energy resources to economic uses also generates significant environmental impacts. These impacts, attendant on coal mining, oil exploration and extraction, fossil fuel combustion, and nuclear power generation have been at the center of the environmental debates of the last century. There is no known means to prevent the buildup of atmospheric carbon dioxide and its anticipated climatic effects if fossil fuel use increases. There are no active repositories or proven means for the permanent isolation of high-level radioactive wastes over thousands of years, despite three decades of nuclear power generation.

These side effects impose significant costs on parties other than the energy users—sometimes across national and generational boundaries. Balancing these costs against the benefits of energy use is the central task of environmental regulation. Few nations have done so with great success internally through national and local regulation. Nor have mechanisms yet been developed to deal effectively with such international side effects as acid rain and the threat of climate change. To the extent that conservation and improved energy efficiency, solar energy, and other relatively benign sources can take the place of fossil fuels and nuclear power, these environmental problems will be mitigated.

The link between energy and global security is another priority issue. Tensions arising from competition for petroleum supplies and the connections between commercial nuclear power development and the proliferation of nuclear weapons are of special concern. The vital interests of the superpowers in assured access to oil imports could cause regional conflicts, like those in the Middle East, to escalate. The large-scale deployment of nuclear power under present international regulation, especially if fuel reprocessing or breeder reactors are commercialized, will enormously widen access to weapons-grade material and decrease the time needed for nonnuclear states to develop nuclear weapons capability.

The main response to these problems should be to promote energy efficiency and conservation—usually the most cost-effective, environmentally benign, and most apt way to reduce international threats and conflicts. Although the price rises of the last decade have stimulated improvements in energy efficiency, enormous opportunities are still available. The apparent oil glut of the past three years has weakened the market incentive to pursue these opportunities. The preeminent goal must be to devise appropriate price signals, which reflect energy scarcities and principal externalities, consistently and over the long term.

Another goal should be to encourage development of renewable energy technologies, including direct solar, wind, hydro, and biomass technologies. Many of these are still on the steep slope of the learning curve and could eventually become competitive over a broad range of uses. A critical policy, of course, is to remove the market biases under which renewable energy sources now suffer, relative to fossil fuels, in many countries.

Achieving Better Energy Efficiency

Although many countries have allowed domestic energy prices to rise toward international levels, there are still widespread subsidies to energy users, both direct and implicit, that weaken incentives to improve energy efficiency. China, for example, with enormous reserves of coal, prices sales for domestic use at a fraction of the export price and burns enormous quantities with very low efficiency and serious environmental side effects. The sensitivity of energy use to price signals, contrary to established wisdom at the time, was demonstrated in the 1970s, as energy use was effectively decoupled from GDP growth. But detailed end-use audits still show enormous unrealized efficiency gains. Despite the past decade's achievements, the worldwide potential is still largely untapped. Pricing reforms are a powerful stimulus to efficiency, even in socialist and mixed economies like China's.

Many petroleum-producing countries such as Mexico, Nigeria, and countries of the Middle East still maintain internal liquid fuel prices well below international levels, although in the past five years considerable progress has been made by other countries such as Indonesia, in eliminating these price distortions. These subsidies lead to rapid growth in the domestic consumption of energy, discourage gains in efficiency, and distort investment decisions. Countries can preserve exportable supplies or reduce import bills, lower production costs, and reduce environmental problems by raising domestic petroleum and natural gas prices at least to international levels.

Petroleum-rich countries often object to this prescription on the grounds that low domestic energy prices stimulate the development of energy-dependent industries, in which their resource endowment provides them a comparative advantage. Often this is a mistake: countries with oil are not necessarily efficient producers of energy-intensive commodities such as metals. The low energy prices can merely provide the illusion of comparative advantage, but better analysis would show that investment would bring higher returns in other sectors. In order to avoid sending a misleading signal, governments can use direct funding or other types of support to encourage energy-intensive undertakings, rather than the indirect means of subsidizing energy prices.

Often such subsidies impose a significant drain on the revenues of government agencies or the treasury. The additional revenues that accrue when subsidies are reduced can, in part, be used to offset the higher energy costs to low-income households, especially through economically sound programs that finance energy conservation programs (for example, through tax rebates or credits) or to provide alternative energy sources (for example, expanded fuelwood plantation programs in developing countries).

In the electric power sector, most countries—including the United States—set prices to yield a return on average costs, which is nowadays often less than the cost of providing additional supplies. Inflation, increasing investment requirements for environmental controls, and slower accumulation of scale economies and technological innovations have reversed the past declines in electricity costs. In addition, many countries also let prices and revenues lag so badly behind cost increases that the electricity supply sector runs at a serious loss. Incremental cost pricing in rate structures ensures that the incentives to consumers to save electricity are as great as the cost of producing more, and also that the incentives to develop alternative energy sources are as high as the costs of the energy that is replaced. Average cost pricing and declining block rates for large users deter conservation.

In many developing countries, fiscal incentives encourage energy-intensive investments. For example, tariff distortions encourage road transport over rail; investment incentives and credit policies encourage capital-intensive over labor-intensive industrialization. Over the long run, a fiscal system (encompassing taxes, tariffs, and interest rates) that promotes rapid employment growth will encourage energy efficiency as well. In this sense, attending to basics, particularly the need for faster job creation, has payoffs in resource and environmental conservation as well.

However, powerful as they are, market incentives are often insufficient to induce users to adopt cost-effective improvements in energy savings because information is lacking, because the investor would not reap the gain, or because in many cases financing is unavailable. The best-known developed-country example is in rental housing: a builder who wants to minimize construction costs to attract customers skimps on energy-saving features; the owner does not pay the energy bills; and the tenant—whose lease and intended stay is relatively short—cannot fully recover the value of energy-saving investments he might make himself. Therefore, the incentives for conservation are weak all around.

Where energy use for space heating and cooling is high, governments can get around this kind of problem by granting tax credits for residential energy savings, providing credits for energy improvements in low-income housing, encouraging involvement of utilities in conservation investments, requiring that thermal performance information be provided when buildings are sold or rented, and by requiring individual metering in multifamily dwellings.

Similar problems arise in the production and sale of major appliances, which account for a substantial share of nonindustrial energy use in developed countries. Purchasers tend to opt for low initial cost, even if the lower energy efficiency means higher costs over the appliance's lifetime—especially if the purchaser is a landlord or contractor. Governments should set performance standards or at least adopt energy-use labeling requirements for major appliances. For the same reason, fuel performance standards and labeling requirements are effective mechanisms for encouraging cost-effective energy savings in cars and trucks.

Institutional barriers often impede energy savings. Utility charters hinder their involvement in conservation activities or the commercial sale of power by cogenerators. Uncertainties exist whether cost savings or profits gained by regulated utilities would be subject to rate-of-return constraints or whether nonutilities getting involved in energy supply would open themselves to government regulation. Legal clarification, such as provided in the United States by PURPA (1978), can open the way for efficient and profitable energy savings and supply innovations. Of particular importance are regulations and laws that facilitate the sale of surplus power to utilities and users by cogenerators at marginal replacement cost.

Utilities or other electricity producers that already exist should be allowed to transform themselves into energy service companies, able to meet energy needs in the most appropriate manner, whether through the sale of electricity or conservation information, equipment or services. Where electricity providers are being created for the first time, this new model should be followed.

Encouraging Renewable Energy Supplies

Numerous assessments show that renewable sources might provide a markedly higher share of total energy over the medium to long term, particularly if increased energy efficiency slows the growth of demand.[18] For many years, the development of renewable sources and their market penetration have been retarded by incentives and other policies favoring fossil fuels. In the United States, for example, the development of nuclear power was encouraged by massive federal expenditures on research, the legal limitation of industry liability for accidents, and other measures that renewable energy industries have not shared. In many developing countries, biomass and solar energy sources are largely outside the commercial sector and have been grossly neglected.

Policies and incentive structures that provide subsidies and other advantages to suppliers of fossil fuels and nuclear power make it impossible for renewable and other nonrenewable sources to compete on an equal footing in all potential markets. The most important and fundamental step that can be taken to ensure that renewable energy sources are appropriately phased in would be to provide a level playing field for competition.

There is a clear-cut need for expanded research and development efforts on solar and biomass conversion technologies. Many of these, such as improved designs for cooking stoves and biogas digesters, cannot readily be patented or marketed privately in developing countries. Like new uses for biological resources, they cannot attract private resource financing. Yet energy ministries devote little of their research funding to developing these technologies. USAID and other aid agencies should expand support for research on renewable energy systems in developing countries, emphasizing in-country research and extension by local institutions.

Managing Environmental Impacts

Most industrial countries have elaborate legal and regulatory frameworks to manage internal environmental damages arising

18. Amulya K. N. Reddy, "Energy Issues and Opportunities," in Repetto, ed., *The Global Possible.*

from energy conversion. However, energy conservation is the most effective and generally the least-cost means of reducing these environmental impacts, and this has not been fully grasped. Even within the regulatory sphere, recent experience has shown that the same degree of protection can be obtained at much lower cost if innovative approaches are adopted. Industrial countries have not yet evolved mechanisms to resolve international and global environmental impacts, such as air and water pollution and possible climatic change. Developing countries, many of which are beginning to encounter acute environmental problems originating in the energy sector, have on the whole not yet established effective control mechanisms.

Innovative regulatory approaches, such as the use of "bubbles" and tradable emissions permits in air pollution control programs, have demonstrated the feasibility of markedly reducing the real costs of environmental protection. Governments in the industrial countries, where public support for protecting the environment is overwhelming, can broaden the use of mechanisms such as these that promote cost-effective abatement of environmental impacts.

Developing countries that are just putting into place basic systems of law, regulation, monitoring, and research for environmental protection have an extraordinary opportunity to learn from the mistakes of the industrial countries and to avoid the costly, litigious, largely ineffectual patchwork of controls that they have evolved through the years. Proper siting and land-use planning can greatly reduce environmental damages and control costs. Policies that emphasize resource savings and recovery in circular production systems and minimize reliance on end-of-pipe emissions controls can avoid shunting wastes from air to water to land and back again. Furthermore, residuals management systems that look at the risks and costs of alternatives comprehensively can achieve much more sensible solutions to the inevitable problems that accompany industrialization.

International agencies, environmental protection agencies in the industrial countries, and training institutions should greatly expand technical assistance programs to strengthen the legal, managerial, and scientific capabilities of the developing countries in dealing with the environmental impacts of energy conversion and other industrial activities so that they can better take advantage of this opportunity.[19]

Energy and Security Issues

Energy dependence on petroleum imports is an important source of international tension and potential conflict. So also is the threat of nuclear proliferation through access to weapons-usable materials from nuclear power facilities or the sabotage of such facilities. Major importers, acting singly or in cooperation, should consider policies that reflect the economic and political risks of heavy import dependence on petroleum, such as an oil import levy. Such a levy with rates that varied countercyclically would tend to stabilize energy prices. Moreover, for the United States, where consumption and import levels are so large as to affect world prices and the behavior of the export cartel, there is a strong economic argument for an import levy that would be borne in substantial part by producers in the form of lower—perhaps considerably lower—OPEC prices.[20] The logical time to impose such a tax is now, when prices are falling and the producers' cartel shows signs of coming unstuck.

A rapid improvement in energy efficiency to take advantage of technologically and economically attractive opportunities could satisfy worldwide demands for energy services while limiting the need for new energy supplies to levels that can be sustained without endangering political or environmental stability. Achievement of this goal through implementation of initiatives such as these will do much to ensure not only a sustainable energy future but also a sustainable human future.

AIR, ATMOSPHERE, AND CLIMATE

Scientists have warned, because of important discoveries during the past decade, that our activities may cause serious changes in

19. Lee M. Talbot, "Helping Developing Countries Help Themselves," World Resources Institute Study for the Environmental and Energy Study Institute (Washington, D.C.: World Resources Institute, January 1985).

20. Elena Folberts-Landau, "The Social Cost of Imported Oil," *The Energy Journal* 5, no. 3 (July 1984): 41–59.

the global atmosphere and climate. Their understanding of the relationship between changes in atmospheric composition, climate, and ecosystems is still modest, but it is known that changes within the range of possibility could produce enormous social and economic dislocations.[21] Acid rain, stratospheric ozone changes due to chlorofluorocarbons (CFCs), and the greenhouse effect are the three most publicized and studied transnational atmospheric problems.

Acids formed from sulfur and nitrogen oxide emissions are deposited in rain, snow, and fog, as well as in dry forms. Coal and oil burned in industrial and utility boilers are the main sources, along with motor vehicle exhausts that contain nitrogen oxides. These acids have already damaged lakes, fish stocks, and buildings in many countries. Norway and Sweden, among others, have documented the loss of fish populations in thousands of lakes. The whole world was shocked to learn that India's Taj Mahal, an architectural masterpiece, was endangered by sulfur emissions from an oil refinery upwind. Acids may also be seriously affecting crops and forests. One-half of West Germany's forests has been damaged by air pollution, and successive surveys have shown the damage to be increasing. Norway spruce, fir, pine, beech, oak, and other trees have died back, with excessive mortality over wide regions. In the United States, declines in growth rates of loblolly and shortleaf pines during the past two decades have been measured throughout the Piedmont region of the Carolinas, Georgia, and Alabama. In the Northeast, red spruce stands show reduced growth and increased mortality, as well as visible damage to needles. Recent studies have shown that forests and lakes in the western states are vulnerable to acidification as well.[22] A great deal of detective work is now going on to discover the reasons and the mechanisms, because the symptoms differ among species and regions. High-elevation forests are often bathed in clouds and fog that contain high concentrations of many aerosols, and forests are known to suffer damage from ozone and other gaseous pollutants.

21. Stephen H. Schneider and Starley L. Thompson, "Future Changes in the Atmosphere," in Repetto, ed., *The Global Possible.*

22. Philip Roth et al., *The American West's Acid Rain Test*, Research Report no. 1 (Washington, D.C.: World Resources Institute, March 1985).

Since emissions sources can be at considerable distances, even in different countries, from the point of deposition, agreements on controls are difficult to obtain. The spreading damage, however, has prompted several governments to greater action, despite the remaining uncertainty over the sources and mechanisms of injury. West Germany, for example, has enacted tough new restrictions on power plant and industrial emissions and is attempting to lead the European Economic Community (EEC) to adopt vehicular emissions standards at the levels mandated in the United States. Although control technologies for both vehicles and large stationary sources are available, increased use of abundant coal resources and growing emissions of nitrogen oxides could exacerbate these problems in Europe and other regions unless governments act.

Although acid deposition is a regional issue, the depletion of stratospheric ozone is a global one. Ozone in the stratosphere shields the earth from ultraviolet (UV) solar radiation. It also influences the temperature of the stratosphere. In the 1970s, scientists determined that the release of chlorine, nitrogen oxides, and other chemicals could catalyze reactions that destroy ozone. CFCs used in aerosol sprays, foam blowing, solvents, and refrigeration are thought to present the greatest risk. Both the United States and the European Economic Community, major producers and consumers of CFCs, have taken steps to curtail their use. The United States banned "inessential" uses in aerosol sprays in 1974, whereas Europe relied on more general controls. However, production and emissions of CFCs and other ozone-depleting gases are projected to continue increasing at an average rate between 1.5 and 4 percent annually, in the absence of effective new controls. A medium projection of 2.5-percent annual growth predicts accelerating ozone depletion, especially after the turn of the century, and a 25-percent reduction in ozone concentrations by the year 2075. Because of the nonlinearity of the underlying atmospheric chemistry, a higher rate of emissions growth would greatly exacerbate the pace and extent of ozone depletion. Significant vertical redistribution of ozone is expected under almost all scenarios, and the models predict significant ozone depletion at high altitudes partially offset by ozone increases at lower altitudes.

Short-wave solar radiation (UV-B) now effectively absorbed by ozone would reach the earth's surface in much greater amounts were the ozone shield depleted. A 25-percent depletion is estimated to raise the numbers of nonmelanoma skin cancers among light-skinned peoples throughout the world by about 3.5 million per year. Certain plant cultivars, aquatic larvae and phytoplankton, and cattle also appear sensitive to UV radiation damage, so that considerable agricultural and ecological damages might result. In the commercial realm, the addition of stabilizers to synthetic materials to counteract the effects of UV-B on product lifetimes might add billions of dollars to worldwide production costs should ozone depletion at this scale occur.

Almost one hundred years ago, scientists first recognized that carbon dioxide emitted by fossil fuel combustion and other trace gases could warm the earth. These chemicals are commonly termed greenhouse gases because they allow the sun's visible radiation to penetrate but block infrared energy radiated back from the earth. The buildup of carbon dioxide in the atmosphere is well documented, and intensive study has not revealed any fatal flaws in the basic theory of greenhouse warming. The current consensus is that under present expectations of fossil fuel use, mean global surface temperatures will have risen by 1.5 to 4.5°C by about the middle of the next century as a result of carbon dioxide buildup alone. Projected changes in other greenhouse gases could approximately double these figures. These changes, larger than any experienced since the last ice age, could have very large impacts on local weather and rainfall. Sea level may rise by two feet or more. The temperature rise will not be uniform in space or time and will affect the climate of some areas much more than others, but efforts to characterize impact by region are still extremely tentative. The temperature of the world's surface has increased in the past century by an amount consistent with the greenhouse theory. The next decade should reveal whether this warming is emerging from the background of natural climatic fluctuations.

Local air quality problems due to industrial activity and use of liquid fuels for transportation are also important from an international perspective. Respiratory disease and other health problems due to air pollution are constant urban problems. There has been considerable progress in stabilizing or reducing smog in the developed world, but similar problems are rapidly emerging in developing nations along with urbanization. Air quality in Seoul, Beijing, Shanghai, Bangkok, Mexico City, and in other major Third World cities is astonishingly bad.

Our overriding objective ought to be avoiding large, irreversible changes in the atmosphere. We should strive to identify the impact of human activities as quickly as possible, in order to minimize the danger of unanticipated harmful changes and to allow the longest possible time for adjustment. The risks associated with a wait-and-see approach may be severe. The potential impact of climatic changes can be mitigated by anticipatory responses such as the planning of flexible and diverse energy supply strategies to allow a decrease in carbon dioxide emissions and the development of flexible agricultural strategies to allow successful adaptation to changes that do occur.

Although large uncertainties remain, there exists sufficient knowledge on atmospheric problems to justify immediate action to hedge against plausible risks. In addition, a commitment to long-term research is needed, both to sharpen our responses and to alert us to other problems as they arise. Research is more likely to be effective and countries are more likely to agree on the nature of the problems if there is regular, extensive scientific exchange. Decisions to implement multilateral measures require some framework for *cooperative policy formulation,* through either an existing multilateral institution or some new arrangement.

The most feasible preventive measures are those that contribute to other environmental and economic goals. Implementing them at the earliest possible time minimizes both the risks of climatic change and the cost of implementing more radical measures in the future. Although policy choices are frequently cast as a balance or battle between the benefits of clearing up the environmental problem under discussion and the costs of abating or changing the offending activity, all the steps required to deal with these atmospheric issues are needed to deal with other environmental and economic problems, so these international-scale atmospheric hazards simply add to the need to face effectively other long-standing problems.

First among these steps are energy conservation and improvements in energy end-use efficiency. The energy initiatives described above outline various steps required to reduce worldwide dependence on petroleum and other fossil fuels. Implementing these also reduces the rate of carbon dioxide buildup and nitrogen oxide emissions and gives us additional time to face the greenhouse and acid rain problems. Similarly, eliminating net deforestation through implementation of the forestry initiatives also eliminates a source of carbon dioxide, and reforestation stores carbon out of the atmosphere.

Among the atmospheric problems themselves, there are additional cross-benefits. Combustion exhausts contain an ugly mix of compounds, many of them toxic even in trace amounts. Not much is known about their joint effects on living things or, for that matter, how they react in the atmosphere to form still other compounds. There is an unfortunate tendency to focus on specific pollutants or particular environmental symptoms as if they were distinct problems. In the United States, for example, there are separate air quality regulations governing concentrations of sulfur dioxide, nitrogen dioxide, suspended particulates, photochemical smog, and lead and also proposed or actual control measures directed at visibility impairment, acid precipitation, respirable particulates, and depletion of stratospheric ozone. Yet all stem in large part from the same smokestacks and exhaust pipes as combustion by-products. Reducing fossil fuel use lowers carbon dioxide output and cuts into all of these problems, and reducing emissions of sulfur and nitrogen compounds cuts into most. Most air pollution cleanup programs reduce one or more greenhouse gases while they achieve their primary purpose.

Much of the recent research on the impact of atmospheric contaminants has been in a crisis-response mode, attempting to develop quick answers to queries from governing bodies about the seriousness of one or another postulated harmful change. A far more effective approach would be to conduct a vigorous and steady program of studies on the nature and processes of the atmosphere. The advantages would be several: (a) with a group constantly at work, earlier insight might be provided into a wide range of possible problems and their interconnections; (b) early studies avoid some of the polarization in policy debates in which scientific uncertainties are used as political weapons; and (c) steady effort is likely to produce a wider range of ideas about preventing, mitigating, and adapting to problems that do arise. Studies that are conceived and executed collaboratively among scientific groups from upwind and downwind countries and that involve interested industrial, government, and academic researchers have an obvious additional value. Recent initiatives such as joint research into acid rain problems between the United Kingdom and Scandinavia or the United States and Canada and international research programs on climate change are indicative of the possibilities in narrowing scientific disagreement. Parallel research on the possibility of nuclear winter by American and Russian scientists is another important example.

One unchanging characteristic of the atmosphere is its changeability. Years can be hot or dry, months can stray far from the norm, and extreme weather affects us in many ways. Variations are like experiments in which we learn of atmospheric processes and test our evolving theories. Extreme events mimic climate change, for which we should be adequately prepared. The steps needed to prepare for such events and to prevent the human suffering they cause are indeed the same steps needed to prepare for or adapt to possible climate change, whether it is induced by greenhouse gases or is driven by such external forces as increased volcanic activity or long-term shifts in the output of the sun.

These interconnections are echoed in the specific initiatives for policy and research described in the sections that follow.

Acid Rain

Decisions to respond to the evidence of spreading damages to forests, lakes, crops, and materials have been delayed by uncertainty over the offending substances and their sources and the pathways and mechanisms that lead to damage. Important research programs have been begun both in Europe and in North America to narrow this uncertainty and to provide a better basis for policy responses that will very likely have to be expensive. These obviously deserve continued priority support and would benefit from a greater degree of intercommunication. At the same time, regulatory studies in Europe and the United States directed toward underlying decisions to impose new emissions standards or controls on vehicular and industrial emissions need to balance *all* the environmental benefits against the costs, not just the reduction in acidic deposition.

An important obstacle to international agreement on additional controls is the high cost and technical problems of flue gas desulfurization systems for large smokestacks and catalytic converters for vehicles. Other potentially superior technologies are being developed that may reduce control costs: for example, advanced fluidized bed combustion systems for coal-fired boilers and improved automotive engines. These developments deserve government support, not only through financial contributions but, perhaps more importantly, through policy decisons that do not freeze technologies but encourage the speedy adoption of new ones if they are advantageous.

The United States and other industrialized countries should seek major reductions in sulfur and nitrogen emissions over the next decade. The EEC, with West Germany in the lead, is actively considering proposals for reductions ranging from 30 to 60 percent of 1980 levels. A variety of measures have been introduced as legislation in the U.S. Congress. Aside from the scientific uncertainties about the effectiveness of such measures, the key issues, of course, are who will reduce emissions and who will pay the bill. Countries or regions that have already gone further in controlling emissions naturally think that others should bear more of the burden, while those that would face heavy costs to reduce damages elsewhere believe the beneficiaries should contribute.

The polluter-pays principle emphasized in OECD environmental studies and endorsed by most economists has the distinct advantage that it places the costs imposed on others through environmental impacts squarely on the activities that generate the damages and, indirectly, on consumers of the products generated by polluting production processes and on the inputs into production. This creates strong incentives to find less-damaging processes and, if that is impossible, to cut back on the scale of the activity when substitutes are available.

Whoever pays, decisions to take action will be more acceptable if the costs are kept to a minimum. Experience with air quality regulations in the past has demonstrated that clumsy and inefficient regulations can double or triple the costs of achieving any air quality goal. Meat-ax approaches that mandate uniform emissions reductions for all sources or adoption of uniform control technologies without regard to differences among sources that greatly affect the cost and efficacy of such measures greatly inflate the total costs. In the United States, more flexible regulations such as emissions trading, which permits firms to substitute greater reductions at sources that are easily controlled for lesser reductions at sources that are expensive to control, has resulted in large savings with no loss of effectiveness. The government of the Netherlands has adopted this concept in its program of reducing sulfur emissions, and the French environmental ministry's program to reduce sulfur emissions by 50 percent during the 1980s includes energy conservation, fuel substitution, and adoption of clean technologies, not just the scrubbing of exhaust gases.

Industrializing Third World countries with large coal reserves—China and Indonesia, for example—may face increasingly severe problems with acidic deposition as well as with local air pollution. Yet the costs of conventional control technologies are intimidating, since they can raise the bill on new power plants by 10 to 15 percent. In such countries, the scope for higher energy efficiencies are great, and the resulting energy savings can reduce the growth rate of demand by as much as half—making the capital cost burden, including environmental controls, easier to bear. One key to achieving these higher efficiencies is better pricing of energy resources. Countries with large domestic deposits tend to price energy too cheaply and thereby encourage very rapid growth of demand.

Such countries can also avail themselves of intermediate technologies that achieve more limited abatement of emissions at considerably lower costs per ton. Coal washing, for example, can often remove 30 to 50 percent of the sulfur before burning, depending on its form in the coal, and the cost per ton of sulfur removed is much less than that with scrubbers, which may remove 80 to 90 percent. Removing half the sulfur cheaply rather than almost all of it at high cost may make sense for a low-income country.

Ozone Depletion

As with acid rain, remaining uncertainties regarding the processes and risks involved are great enough to deter action. Efforts to detect ozone changes and test theories of ozone depletion by satellite measurements, balloon tests, and other field research should be expanded. More research is needed on the effects of UV radiation on immunological processes, photosynthesis, and marine life. The climate change induced by the altered vertical stratospheric temperature distribution should also be studied. However, the potential risks of ozone depletion and the relatively modest perceived costs of prevention made this the first instance of an international anticipatory response to a global environmental problem. The United States banned the use of CFCs in nonessential uses, and European nations took steps to reduce their use also.

The convention for the protection of the ozone layer is a good example of a framework for international negotiations and agreement on measures to control a problem of international scope. The UNEP has played a valuable role in sponsoring and organizing the process of negotiations. However, the negotiations stalled in early 1985 without agreement on measures to reduce CFC production and use. Delegates were divided over two equally flawed proposals. The United States proposes, with some variants, that all countries ban inessential uses of CFCs, particularly aerosol propellants for hair sprays and the like. This has been the U.S. approach domestically. The European Economic Community basically advocates a limit on production of CFCs at current capacity levels. Current negotiations seek an acceptable blend of these two proposals.

The flaws in the U.S. proposal are, first, that it does not adequately limit nonaerosol CFC uses as refrigerants, solvents, and foaming agents. These uses have grown and would continue to increase. Second, it puts environmental ministries in the uncomfortable censorious position of socioeconomic arbiters, deciding what uses are essential and inessential. The flaws in the EEC proposal are that it fails to encourage any phasing out of CFCs until capacity limits are reached, which—given current levels of overcapacity—would not be likely until the next century. Also, when current capacity limits are reached, it invites producers to establish new capacities in nonsignatory countries, while developing countries that do sign are perpetually limited to a small share of the market.

Unfortunately, parties to the negotiation have not yet considered the use of a pricing mechanism to limit CFC use, despite its advantages. If all signatory countries agreed to adopt a uniform ad valorem excise tax, applicable equally to domestic production and imports, CFC use and production would be discouraged, there would be no need to distinguish inessential uses, and low-cost producers could still enter the market. Inessential uses, for which either cheap substitutes exist or demand is readily cut back, would identify themselves: price increases due to the tax would drive them out of the market. Further, the higher prices would continually prompt users and producers to find substitutes. The pattern of production would not be frozen: efficient producers would still satisfy the remaining demands, and high-cost producers would cut back on output. With the information on production costs and uses that has already been gathered, it would not be difficult to estimate the level of the tax needed to achieve the desired reduction in production.

The Greenhouse Effect

The distinct possibility of having to accommodate a climate warming justifies a substantial research effort to understand the processes at work and their possible effects. Research on how the oceans and the biosphere act as sources or sinks for carbon dioxide should be greatly expanded, along with research on the effect of and release rates for greenhouse gases other than carbon dioxide. The quality of the global monitoring network should be improved, with more stations and increased efforts to obtain consistent, reliable data for many more chemicals and for temperatures over the oceans and in remote areas.

Joint regional programs should investigate the regional implications of increases in global mean temperature. Research on the synergistic effects of multiple environmental stresses on human health and ecosystems is urgently needed. Essentially none is being done on the possible interactions between UV radiation, carbon dioxide, drought, and other factors.

The possible adverse effects of significant climate change underscore the advantages of energy conservation and efficiency improvements, flexibility and diversity of supply, and increased reliance on solar and other noncarbonaceous energy sources (with due attention to the other environmental problems that using these alternatives might entail). Further, the steps outlined above to stem the tragic global deforestation now under way and to promote reforestation efforts will protect climate. The world's forests and soil humus hold large amounts of carbon, and converting forests to other uses releases much of the carbon as carbon dioxide.

Government discussion of global atmospheric problems has been slow to develop. Scientific uncertainties, along with economic and political factors, have made it impossible, with few exceptions, to agree on a cooperative policy response. Official exchanges of scientific information are often slow, and information flows within a discipline rather than among several. Communication with the centrally planned economies and developing countries, particularly important for addressing these issues, has also not always been effective or frequent. UNEP's Climate Impact Study Program and the World Meteorological Organization's World Climate Program, created to promote greater international understanding of climate and atmospheric processes, could play a greater role. It may now be possible to create a mechanism or framework for discussing the need for and types of policy initiatives. The Framework Convention for the Protection of the Ozone Layer is a possible model.

OCEANS AND MARINE LIVING RESOURCES

The oceans play a central role in the biological, chemical, and physical cycles on which life depends. Evaporation from the oceans renews the hydrologic cycle that provides our fresh waters. The oceans are a vast reservoir of carbon and regulate atmospheric buildup of carbon dioxide. Similarly, the oceans are immense sinks and ultimate sources of nitrogen, sulfur, phosphorus, and other elements. The oceans moderate and greatly influence weather patterns.

Until very recently, the view prevailed that the marine environment would take care of itself. Marine and coastal ecosystems do have a substantial ability to cleanse themselves and stay productive, but today, at least in estuaries, bays, and semienclosed seas, their absorptive and rejuvenative capacities have been surpassed. For example, a 1983 assessment of the status of Chesapeake Bay, one of the world's most productive estuaries, concluded that most of it is overloaded with nutrients and that as a result, the volume of water depleted of oxygen in the summer has increased fifteenfold during the past 30 years; that heavy metals and organic toxics contaminate much of its bottom sediments; and that its living resources—especially those that depend on fresh water as juveniles—are at an all-time low.

Scientific understanding of the oceans is rudimentary. Knowledge of the reasons for both positive and negative changes is still extremely limited. Exploitive uses of marine resources can and will continue, but the more scientists know, the more they emphasize the need for caution and restraint.

Fisheries Management

At one time, fish were thought to be an inexhaustible resource. However, it is now understood that although oceans cover nearly three-fourths of the earth's surface, harvestable marine resources are limited because much of the ocean is infertile and nearly all primary production is carried out by microscopic and submicroscopic plants. Typically, neither the plants nor the animals that prey directly on them are big enough to harvest. Most marine fisheries exploit carnivores high on the food chain and, because at least three-fourths of available energy is lost at each step up the food chain, the amount of energy stored in harvestable stocks is low.

Since the balance of nature keeps the stocks of species constant, at least on average, garnering harvestable surpluses without depleting those stocks has until now required changing the age distribution in favor of young, rapidly growing individuals. Other ways of manipulating the ecosystem, such as removing predators and competitors and improving the genetic properties of exploited stocks so that they yield more of the products desired by people— the strategies of agriculture—have not been brought much into play in the oceans.

The reason, of course, is the open-access, common-property organization of most of the world's fisheries, which deters private investments except in equipment for catching and processing the fish. It is noteworthy that in those few fisheries that have established property rights, such as the Atlantic oyster grounds leased to private oystermen, productivity has risen rapidly through such simple measures as excluding predators like starfish and crabs and improving the beds.

The other consequence of open access is overexploitation, and today the world is faced with many depleted fish stocks. Overfishing is the main threat, but habitat destruction and coastal pollution have become major concerns. The result of past and present overfishing is that the annual world catch is fifteen to twenty million tons—about 20 percent—lower than it might otherwise have been, and at least twenty-five of the world's most valuable fisheries are seriously depleted. Many depleted fisheries may never be rehabilitated, because species of commercial importance are replaced in their ecological niches by other species of limited usefulness.[23]

Some of the seriously depleted stocks are in inshore coastal fisheries in the developing countries that provide livelihoods for millions of poor families. Although mechanizing the boats only accelerates overfishing, investments in hatcheries, basic refrigeration facilities, and processing plants near landing points can raise the fishermen's incomes. These overcrowded inshore fisheries can often be relieved only through programs to expand alternative employment opportunities. Small-scale aquaculture operations can greatly raise the productivity of artisanal fishermen.

In the aggregate, between 10 and 20 percent of the world fish

23. Roger Revelle, "Present and Future State of Living Marine and Freshwater Resources," in Repetto, ed., *The Global Possible.*

catch is wasted. In some developing countries, losses, including spoilage, can run as high as 40 percent. Incidental take of unwanted species is responsible for the destruction and waste of more than seven million tons a year, about 10 percent of the total catch. The incidental take also threatens the extinction of several species of sea turtles and has led to greater catches of cetaceans (especially dolphins and porpoises) than occurs through intentional harvesting. This waste and destruction can be reduced if fishing nations regulate fishing nets appropriately and operate storage ships so the incidental catch can be transferred.

Although regulation of fish catches is beginning to limit overfishing, degradation of coastal habitats threatens to be an even greater problem if existing trends continue. More than 70 percent of the world's population lives in coastal areas. Unfortunately, all too often development actions in coastal areas fail to balance the needs for protection, conservation, and sustainable use. Some of the degradation is caused by pollution. Discharges from the land are by far the most significant sources, and because they are a regular by-product of dispersed daily activities, too little is known about their fate or impacts. It is possible to protect ecologically vital areas, such as estuaries and wetlands, from land-based pollution by enforcing controls over sediment runoff from construction, discharge of toxic materials into drainage channels and sewers, and limitations on the discharge of agricultural chemicals into watercourses.

The rest—and probably the greater source of stress—is the result of physical modification of coastal areas. The destruction of mangroves and coastal wetlands has eliminated important marine nurseries. The problem is serious because 60 to 80 percent of commercially valuable marine fishery species use wetlands, estuaries, and other areas near the ocean shorelines as spawning, nursery, and foraging grounds at some point in their life cycles.

Given all this, increasing total harvests much above the present level of about seventy million metric tons per year will be difficult. Some gains can be expected from (a) better exploitation of some stocks in the southern oceans, (b) harvesting lower down in the food chain (especially by commercially exploiting krill, the abundant crustaceans of the southern oceans), (c) exploiting some of the fishes that live further below the ocean surface than those normally harvested, and (d) expanding use of such important mollusks as squid. These activities will require new fishing techniques and changes in tastes. Such obstacles are not insurmountable, but even full exploitation of these additional resources is unlikely to increase total harvests much beyond one hundred million metric tons per year.

Great potential exists, however, to increase the efficiency of harvesting of marine resources by moving away from the currently predominant single-species management schemes to ecosystem management schemes. Most productive marine systems contain a number of fish species with broadly overlapping diets. Exploitation of one may increase populations of some others. Since these species are likely to differ in their market value, economic yields can be increased by clever manipulation of competitive relationships. However, because exploited species may also occur at several levels on the food chain within the same community, exploitation at lower levels may markedly influence harvest at higher levels. Fisheries management should devote much greater attention to these ecosystem management concepts.

In marked contrast to the limited expansion potential of traditional fisheries, marine resources can be increased significantly through the development of aquaculture. Aquaculture is limited by current technologies to a narrow coastal strip, a zone under strong pressure from many different potential users. Aquaculture can be competitive with other uses because, under favorable conditions, yields of as much as ten metric tons of fish per hectare per year can be obtained. Aquacultural production is now increasing worldwide at a rate of about 7 percent per year, and thirty million hectares, ten times the present area, could be developed during the coming decades.

A number of problems need to be solved to permit rapid development of aquaculture. Especially needed are research on fish nutrition and diseases and on methods of preserving, processing, and marketing the products. Rapid expansion also requires capital and training in aquaculture techniques, especially in developing countries. Property rights problems in areas now considered part of the public domain can be resolved by enabling potential aquaculturists to lease offshore areas and clarifying their rights to protection against pollution losses. An important step would be the addition of an aquaculture research unit to the Consultative Group on International Agricultural Research.

The Exclusive Economic Zone

Of the 137 independent coastal states in the world, 93 have asserted 200-mile fishing limit claims, and 58 of those have asserted broader claims to EEZs. Within its EEZ, a coastal state has sovereign rights over all marine resources, living (subject to certain conservation standards) and nonliving; has control of virtually all economic uses within that zone, excepting navigation; and has jurisdiction to regulate marine research and protect the marine environment. This recent shift toward enclosure of the coastal zone through the EEZ concept has created an opportunity to put in place new management and conservation approaches.

More than 130 nations have signed the Law of the Sea (LOS) Convention, and at least nine of the sixty ratifications required for its entry into force have been deposited. The Convention's articles establish standards and obligations for the control of pollution from all sources affecting the EEZ, as well as for the conservation of living marine resources, and sound strategies for use and management of the oceans as a whole. Despite the serious problems surrounding the seabed mining provisions and governance provisions of the Convention, these articles are valuable and worth preserving.

Although the promulgation of EEZs has removed nearly 40 percent of the ocean from open-access property status, many developing countries lack resources for monitoring, protecting, and exploiting the marine resources now under their control. This new management opportunity cannot be grasped unless nations build the institutions, expertise, and procedures to ensure the sustainable use of the EEZ. International cooperation in the exchange of data (for example, the global Musselwatch program) and the establishment of internationally compatible, coordinated data banks is a high priority. The Regional Seas Program is a successful model of efforts to secure cooperation among neighboring oceanic states.

Technical assistance can play a valuable role in training scientific and technical personnel, transferring appropriate technology for research and monitoring, and providing expert advice on the development of laws and administrative structures. This technical aid can also help developing countries obtain increased economic benefits from the EEZ through imaginative use of market mechanisms, such as the auction of harvest rights and joint ventures with more advanced fishing nations.

The Antarctic

The Antarctic and its seas will become more important in the coming decades. Antarctica is one of the last places on earth where wildlife can be found at population levels close to their orignal abundance in nearly pristine ecosystems. It is the home of many species that are now threatened in other parts of the world. Antarctic seas are among the most biologically productive in the world. The southern ocean is unique, as one tiny crustacean krill species serves as the foundation species for the entire marine ecosystem. Commercial interest in krill began in the early 1970s, and the annual yield now is believed to be close to one million tons. There is also a significant finfish harvest.

The Antarctic Treaty has provided the primary legal framework for decision making in the region since 1959.[24] Seven of its sixteen signatories claim portions of the continent, but the other nine do not recognize those claims. In 1980, fifteen governments concluded the Convention on the Conservation of Antarctic Marine Living Resources (CCAMLR), which entered into force in 1982. CCAMLR employs an innovative conservation standard, which states that harvesting decisions should take into account possible impacts on dependent species—sometimes referred to as the ecosystem as a whole principle. At this stage, so little is known about the region's ecology that fisheries should be managed on an experimental basis only, with an initial conservative quota by area and appropriate quota enforcement. Feeding grounds of threatened

24. Jonathan I. Charney, ed., *The New Nationalism and the Use of Common Spaces* (Allenheld, N.J.: 1982).

and endangered whales should be identified and closed to krill fishing, and at least one large sanctuary should be established where krill harvesting would be prohibited or permitted only for scientific purposes.

Negotiations currently are under way to complete a new agreement to govern minerals exploitation, which ought to protect the Antarctic from such activities until the environmental risks have been assessed and safeguards developed. The Treaty parties resist revising their current arrangements, because Antarctica's potential resources have become more evident. Where stewardship by the signatories of the Antarctic environment went unchallenged in the past, nations not party to the Treaty and public constituencies are now demanding proof that this charge is being executed responsibly.

Today, the Antarctic is a region in transition. Intellectual curiosity, pure science, and adventure drove early expeditions, but political motives, living resources, and the lure of potential mineral resources have sparked more recent interest. Managing the Antarctic in ways that will maintain the intrinsic values of the Antarctic environment for humankind and the global ecosystem puts special challenges and responsibilities before the Antarctic Treaty Consultative Parties (ATCPs).

It is important that they, in consultation with appropriate international organizations and private voluntary organizations should develop long-term, broadly focused cooperative research programs to investigate the ecological structure and processes of the Antarctic environment and its role with regard to such global phenomena as weather and climate. Against this backdrop, it will be feasible to develop mechanisms to investigate proposed activities—including research and tourism—prepare environmental guidelines, and to monitor operations.

Thereafter, the ATCPs, in consultation with appropriate international organizations, should expand the network of sites meriting special protection. The Biosphere Reserve Program of the Man and the Biosphere Program involves setting aside representative samples of all the earth's major ecosystems and could be the vehicle for conserving Antarctica's unique ecosystems.

NONFUEL MINERALS

Availability and supplies of nonfuel minerals need not seriously limit world economic growth and welfare in the medium or even the long term. Statistics that measure mineral reserves as equal to so many years of consumption are fundamentally misleading, because exploration and discovery add to reserves, and innovation changes both the costs of mineral production and the availability of substitutes. Technological changes have allowed the average grade of copper ore mined in the United States to fall from about 5 percent in 1900 to 0.7 percent today, but copper prices nonetheless fell; strip mining with large earth-moving equipment and the discovery of froth flotation made low-grade ores economical to exploit and greatly increased reserves that were economical to exploit. For example, world consumption of copper between 1950 and 1980 has been 56 percent more than the level of reserves in 1950, but copper has not been used up. On the contrary, world reserves in 1980 were nearly 500 percent of their 1950 level. Known reserves of most other minerals have also increased over time, despite growing consumption.[25]

Economic scarcities, as measured by real prices, have been declining for most nonfuel minerals during the industrial age. That is not to say that declining prices are inevitable. The direction of price changes depends on the results of a race between falling extraction costs and falling ore quality. The prices of most nonfuel minerals seem to be declining at a decreasing rate, and the prices of some, such as iron, nickel, and tin, have started to increase.[26] Technological innovation in extraction, substitutions in use, and the development of new supply sources should moderate price increases. Gradually rising prices are no cause for alarm, because there are ample opportunities for substitution among minerals in

25. William Vogely, "Nonfuel Minerals and the World Economy," in Repetto, ed., *The Global Possible.*

26. Margaret E. Slade, "Trends in Natural Resource Commodity Prices: An Analysis of the Time Domain," *Journal of Environmental Economics and Management* 9, no. 2 (June 1982): 122–137.

most uses, and the importance of minerals in industrial economies—as indicated by consumption per dollar of GDP—has been
declining.

Strengthening World Markets

This relatively optimistic assessment could be overturned,
however, if adjustments by suppliers or consumers are impeded
by barriers to exploration and exploitation of new deposits, by
serious obstacles to the flow of financial capital in the minerals
industry to Third World countries, or by market restrictions by
consumers. The first problem, therefore, is to preserve and
strengthen the conditions for the efficient functioning of minerals
markets, encompassing exploration, investment, extraction, processing, trade, recycling, and ultimate disposal.

Free markets clearly do not solve all resource problems and
sometimes even exacerbate them. Nevertheless, price ceilings imposed by consumer countries in the past have prolonged and exacerbated scarcities and are the most likely source of future crises
in the supply of nonfuel minerals.

In the interests of long-term solutions, international organizations like the United Nations Committee on Trade and Development (UNCTAD), private industries, and governments should
vigorously oppose both cartelization of minerals markets by producers and trade restrictions imposed by importing countries. Instead of counterproductive attempts to promote even more
restrictions on world trade than already exist, UNCTAD and others
should work for a more open and competitive international regime
for trade, investment, and technology flows.

Supply Vulnerability

For major importing countries, an intermediate- and short-term
problem is potential insecurity of supplies of strategic minerals.
Vulnerability stems from reliance on one or few potentially unstable suppliers for materials that are critical to continued defense
or industrial production in emergency situations. There are few
countries that are extremely vulnerable, in this sense, in nonfuel

minerals, and only a short list of critical materials, mainly cobalt, chromium, manganese, and the platinum group. South Africa, Zaire, and the Soviet Union account for more than one-half of world production of these four minerals. Even in these, most current uses are not strategic in the major importing countries, and alternative sources of potential supply exist (including recovery and recycling).[27] The Soviet Union, in fact, placed an embargo on exports of chromium and manganese to the United States, as part of the Berlin crisis of 1948 and 1949. In this, as in other incidents, there were no serious effects on industrial and defense production: world trade patterns were merely reshuffled, which is the usual result of trade embargos. Even vulnerable countries have room to maneuver if regular supplies are interrupted.

Stockpiles have been a reasonable response to concerns about supply interruptions in importing countries and can also serve to mitigate price fluctuations. However, unless their objectives and operating rules are clearly spelled out and adhered to, official stockpiles soon fall prey to producer interests and become devices for holding supplies off the market and prices up—at the expense of consumers and taxpayers.

Producing countries can also use stockpiles as a means of ensuring supplies or stabilizing prices, especially if physical interruptions of production or shipment are important risks. But since producer interests are likely to be even stronger, the risks are greater that they will become a permanent albatross.

Price Instability

Most minerals markets are subject to short-term price instability and cyclical fluctuations. Among the most important reasons are the ease of entry to the market when new sources are found, the heavy potential impact of technological change, and inelastic demand and supply relations. Demands respond slowly to price changes because minerals are intermediate materials embodied in much more expensive final products, and substitutions

27. U.S. Congress, Office of Technology Assessment, *Strategic Minerals: Technologies to Reduce US Import Vulnerability* (Washington, D.C.: January 1985).

involve technological changes with considerable lead times. Supplies also respond sluggishly to price changes because fixed investment costs are a large fraction of total costs, and there are long lead times for normal exploration and development of new deposits.

Modest fluctuations in price trends should not have a substantial impact on aggregate world output. Spot market prices for many minerals are unstable precisely because the bulk of world production is governed by long-term contracts or vertically integrated enterprises—institutional forms that minimize the risks of price instability.

Price instability may increase during the next decade as the importance of vertically integrated multinational firms in mineral markets decreases and that of state enterprises rises, since the latter tend to destabilize prices by overproducing when demand is weak. Wide price swings interfere with planning and—in the case of highly dependent exporting countries—destabilize the balance of payments, internal prices, and government revenues.

In view of the inherent fluctuation of the minerals markets, it is particularly important that conditions of exploration, investment, extraction, and marketing not be additionally destabilized by highly changeable government intervention in regulatory and fiscal matters. A stable policy framework has value in itself because it facilitates planning by producers and consumers, and by governments as well.

However, for countries heavily dependent for foreign exchange earnings and revenues on one or two commodities, price instability is a problem of macroeconomic adjustment. Over the longer term, they can encourage export diversification through appropriate tax, exchange rate, and investment policies. Dutch disease, which stifles other industrial sectors under the overwhelming comparative advantage of the exploitation of some resource, can be combated by differential incentives that make other investments profitable. The World Bank and other aid agencies play a helpful role in assisting export diversification through structural adjustment loans and assistance in carrying out appropriate investment plans.

The past decade has taught international bankers and economic ministers hard lessons about the macroeconomic implications of resource price instability. Many oil exporters followed destabilizing policies during the oil booms, incurring large international debts and expenditure commitments and building insufficient financial reserves. When oil prices fell, these policies turned a difficult adjustment into an international crisis.

Producing countries particularly dependent on revenues from minerals should establish reserve funds that would be built up during high-price periods and could supplement government income in periods of low prices. These reserve policies are essential to macroeconomic stability and can succeed if guided by the long-term price trends of a mineral rather than its short-term price fluctuation.

International financial flows can also help in maintaining macroeconomic stability. The member countries should support an expansion of the International Monetary Fund's (IMF) Compensatory Finance facility to enable exporting countries subject to instability to even out fluctuations in revenues and foreign exchange receipts. For all but the very largest producers, stability must be found through fiscal and monetary policies, not through price stabilization operations in international mineral markets.

Developing Country Benefits

Many developing countries look to revenues from mineral exploitation as an important source of development funds and to mineral processing industries as a spur to industrial growth. Managing mineral resources to accomplish these objectives has been a considerable problem, largely because vertically integrated multinational firms have controlled technology, capital, and markets and because fiscal systems in advanced industrial countries have often discouraged processing beyond primary reduction in the country of origin.

However, it is not an insuperable problem. Host countries can quickly gain the expertise they need by investing a reasonable fraction of projected revenues from minerals development in staff training, consulting services, and agencies to monitor performance under concessions agreements. Technical assistance from the United Nations Development Program (UNDP), the World Bank, and other sources is available for preinvestment work, negotiation of concession agreements, and training of staff in the host countries.

To ensure an adequate and stable flow of investment capital for exploration and exploitation to developing countries, the World Bank, International Finance Corporation (IFC), and government agencies in the investing countries could usefully expand cofinancing and loan guarantee facilities, improve political risk insurance, and increase support for resource identification surveys and preinvestment studies.

Private industry and financing agencies could likewise support unbundling of foreign direct investment (that is, separate supply agreements for capital, technology, management, and marketing) to increase the options available to producing countries in the developing world.

Importing countries, including the newly industrializing nations, should reduce the escalation of tariffs and relax nontariff barriers to fabricated and processed mineral products to enable developing country exporters to increase their value added in the minerals sector. This is the kind of trade-increasing step from which both parties gain. The importing country, over time, reduces resources invested in relatively inefficient—and often environmentally damaging—processing activities, while efficient exporting countries gain additional jobs and income.

Environmental Risks

Mineral exploitation causes environmental damages during extraction, processing, use, and disposal. Mining wastes and conflicting land uses are salient environmental problems of extraction. The processing stage tends to be energy intensive and highly polluting. Both processing and fabrication often generate highly toxic by-products.

The advanced industrial economies have created legislative and regulatory structures to deal with such environmental problems, albeit with difficulty. Developing countries are currently attempting to put in place comparable mechanisms. Although the balance between environmental protection and cost minimization tends to differ between the two, it is unlikely that differential environmental legislation will cause widespread industrial relocation, except possibly in some nonferrous metals industries.

Countries with minerals resources should seek to resolve environmental and land use conflicts by (a) establishing reasonable standards for restoration of mining sites and prevention of off-site pollution, (b) establishing compensatory set-aside policies that preserve equivalent areas for recreational or wilderness use to compensate for all mining sites developed, and (c) establishing policies that exclude highly sensitive or valuable areas from mineral development.

Producing countries should also invest a reasonable fraction of projected revenues from minerals development in staff, services, and facilities to monitor and regulate environmental impacts, to design and evaluate environmental assessments, and to mitigate environmental impacts. Private enterprises in the minerals industries have a strong interest in cooperating with environmental agencies in developing countries, in planning impact assessments and control of environmental damages, and in devising reasonable and effective regulatory systems. Cooperation is more beneficial in the long run to all parties than adversarial relations.[28]

The polluter-pays principle in establishing requirements for site restoration, compensatory set-asides, liability for environmental damages, and control of waste streams assigns responsibility to the party that generally has greater information about risks and control options, and it accurately places the social costs of mineral development on the industry and its customers. It is a sound principle on which to build environmental safeguards in minerals development.

Recycling also has a firm place in minerals policy. It presents an alternate source of monopoly and is subject to the general pressures of the minerals market. It also serves to reduce the waste stream arising from the use of nonfuel minerals and creates benefits that need to be adequately recognized, in particular through

28. Charles S. Pearson, *Down to Business: Multinational Corporations, the Environment and Development*, Study 2 (Washington, D.C.: World Resources Institute, January 1985).

assistance in overcoming institutional barriers to recycling, particularly in the collection of recyclable materials. Governments can promote recycling by examining tax and tariff structures to eliminate biases against secondary materials markets and recovery.

CHAPTER FIVE

Conclusion: Concerted Efforts

The preceding pages have outlined powerful mechanisms for improved resource management and extensive policy agendas to deal with specific resource challenges. These agendas are based on tested and successful experience, and—if carried through—will do much to ensure that the next century sees strong and sustainable progress in building a world that is more secure, more prosperous, and more sustainable both economically and environmentally. But to quote from the concluding statement released by participants in the Global Possible Conference, "These goals will be realized only if a concerted effort is made, with some urgency, to change many current policies and to strengthen and multiply the successful initiatives that already have been undertaken. . . . It will require new levels of cooperation among government, science, business, and groups of concerned people. And it will require a global partnership between developed and developing countries with sustained improvements in the living standards of the world's poor."

IMPLICATIONS FOR THE BUSINESS COMMUNITY

These issues of resource and environmental management raise significant questions for private business, from multinational corporations to small entrepreneurships in developing nations: how

127

can the business community be made more aware that it is in its interest to solve problems of population growth, resource depletion, and environmental damage, and how can it overcome the perception of business as a hostile causal agent of these ills and join with others in seeking solutions to environmental and economic problems?

Global resource issues will probably not be successfully addressed without the support and cooperation of business. Large international companies have the technology and management expertise for successful environmental and resource management. The business community also has obvious long-run interests in the sustained productivity of the resource base. The forest industry, for example, is a primary victim of acid rain and other airborne pollutants, and the fishery industry suffers greatly from land-based water pollution. Improved energy efficiency throughout the economy results in lower energy prices to industrial energy consumers. All businesses, large and small, depend on adequate resources, accessible markets, and social stability. Without these conditions, private enterprise on any scale cannot flower and may not survive.

Therefore, a consensus on goals can be reached among private business, environmentalists, and those most concerned with alleviating poverty. Each group seeks a better standard of living in ways that limit adverse impacts on the biosphere. In the long term, the goal of each must be an ecologically sustainable level of economic activity that satisfies the reasonable aspirations of the world's population. The experience of the past decade suggests that there is no necessary contradiction between economic development and a sustainable resource base.

Although the market mechanisms that determine business behavior are often imperfect in taking into account the external effects of economic activity, the operation of prices and markets is fundamental to economic progress, and private business becomes ineffective if this is distorted or rendered inoperative. The world's total wealth creation will depend on open trading systems among nations. Business must resist the temptation to support domestic and international trade barriers that confer temporary local immunity from competition at the expense of long-term world benefit.

To the extent that externalities can be incorporated into the market equation, business becomes more efficient. The business community can take an expanded, constructive role, especially in developing countries, in promoting legal and regulatory frameworks, encompassing tax and financial policies as well as administrative regulations, that establish incentives and disincentives for the individual business consistent with sustainable resource use.

Private business must be expected to be hardheaded in its assessment of risk and reward, and not philanthropic in its attitude. Yet there are substantial opportunities for the development and sale of more environmentally benign technologies and more efficient ways of resource use, and these represent potentially important markets for business enterprises.

Whether local or multinational, business will, by its nature, gravitate to profitable opportunities, and all over the world businesses are already engaged in marketing energy conservation devices and services and developing renewable energy sources, sustained-yield forestry, bioengineering products for agricultural application, aquaculture, and activities based on resource recovery. Such pursuits will be enhanced by tax and price policies that reconcile private and social returns to investment and a supportive and stable framework of governmental regulations.

To perform its role effectively, private business needs certain conditions, some of which it must help to create. One is an effectively operating public sector, which in most countries has heavy responsibilities for environmental management as well as the provision of core infrastructure and services. Business organizations should increase their efforts to share environmental planning and management skills with government agencies. There are large needs and opportunities for expanded consulting services, especially through joint ventures with developing country firms, in energy management, urban environmental management, and other areas. Much more can also be done to transfer environmental management skills to Third World personnel in the course of investment activities and operations by training local staff and associating more closely with government agencies in environmental assessments.

The business community can contribute more forcefully to the development of improved foresight capability and public awareness of important resource and environmental implications of economic trends. Private sector organizations should examine the resource and environmental implications of their medium- and long-run business projections and join with government and research institutions in providing for the collection and evaluation of relevant data for long-term forecasting. Where legal systems permit, business should consider means of reporting on social and environmental performance as they now report on financial performance.

IMPLICATIONS FOR PRIVATE VOLUNTARY ASSOCIATIONS

In creating public awareness of pressing environmental concerns and political support for the policy agendas that have emerged from the Global Possible Conference, NGOs have a critical role. Leadership will not come from politicians, bureaucrats, and policy analysts, but from the people, as it has in the peace movement, the women's movement, and the environmental movement thus far. One key to action is widespread change in perceptions and values, to which, in most countries, governments respond. Private voluntary associations are in the vanguard of these changes.

There is considerable difficulty in awakening public concern over threats to sustainability that are in the future and to environmental damages that are not yet obvious. Many of the most profound environmental changes that are now under way—climate change, loss of biological resources, depletion of petroleum resources—are largely in that category. Broadening public awareness and concern over such issues is the primary task of the nongovernmental community. Especially important are reaching and involving young people, who are the leaders of the future, because it is their world that is at stake. NGOs should continue to build public concern over long-term, global, or potentially irreversible threats to natural systems, such as degradation of agricultural lands, pollution and depletion of groundwater resources, emergence of resistance to pesticides, loss of tropical forests, depletion of stratospheric ozone, and continuing high rates of population growth. With respect to such issues as the effects of greenhouse gases on climate and the depletion of stratospheric ozone, an important function for nongovernmental institutions is interpreting and presenting the results of scientific research to local communities, regional authorities, and business groups.

Public support is more readily mobilized when a program of feasible and effective action is presented. Warnings of impending threats unconnected to possible solutions often generate fatalism and resignation. There is considerable evidence that solutions are available and have been employed with success by communities and nations. NGOs can build public awareness of the existence and efficacy of these successful policies and mechanisms and help to diffuse them rapidly through international networks of like-minded associations and into other regions and contexts where they might be employed.

Private voluntary associations have been remarkably successful in promoting innovative technologies, production systems, policies, and organizational approaches. Organic farming, solar energy, the delivery of family planning and basic health care services, and irrigation users' associations are just a few of many important examples. Their ability to assume risks and experiment with innovative ideas and their relative independence of past technological and policy commitments puts NGOs in the vanguard of change. By emphasizing experiments and demonstrations of innovative technologies and approaches to sustainable development, including social mechanisms for the management of common resources, voluntary associations can quicken the pace of change.

For most Third World countries, the foremost priority during the past twenty-five years has been the establishment and strengthening of their national economies. Questions of sustainability and resource preservation have been, at best, secondary. NGOs have an even more vital role to play in the Third World in building popular awareness and support. Some of these organizations have remarkable records of achievement at the local, regional, and national levels. Yet they often need financial support from abroad and can benefit from international collaboration and exchange. In turn, NGOs in industrial nations can learn from Third World counterparts, especially about ways of living in harmony with nature. NGOs in the industrial countries should greatly expand their contacts and cooperative activities with counterpart organizations in other regions, especially in the Third World.

IMPLICATIONS FOR THE SCIENTIFIC COMMUNITY

Consideration of virtually all the important environmental and resource issues is hampered by critical gaps in understanding, sometimes sufficiently broad to deter action. The highest priorities for expanded research efforts appear, ironically, both at the largest scale of human interaction with the natural environment and at the smallest. Much more needs to be done to understand global natural systems and the human impact oñ them. At the same time, more research is urgently needed on technologies and production systems, mostly small-scale, that are relevant and useful to the world's poor.

Illustrative of the research needed to understand better human impacts on the global environment are

> more reliable multidimensional models of the atmosphere, including the atmosphere/oceans interactions, and better understanding of the oceans and biosphere as sources or sinks for carbon dioxide
>
> the effects of greenhouse gases other than carbon dioxide on climate
>
> tests of ozone depletion theories and models through satellite and balloon measurement
>
> better understanding of the effects of UV radiation on immunological processes, photosynthesis, and marine life
>
> synergistic effects of multiple environmental stresses, such as UV radiation, enhanced carbon dioxide concentrations, and drought on plant life and human health
>
> effects of acid deposition on agriculture, forest resources, and soil organisms
>
> greatly expanded research into the nature, uses, habitats, and ecological niches of little-known and unknown biological resources.

Examples of the need to develop improved production systems and technologies to raise the productivity and sustainability of the human ecology of the world's poor include

> improved small-scale solar and biomass energy conversion technologies

ecologically sustainable production systems to increase the
productivity of marginal forest lands and arid and semiarid
lands and hilly uplands

crop varieties resistant to climatic stresses such as salinity and
drought and to pests

improved fast-growing, soil-enhancing multipurpose tree species

improved fish species suitable for aquaculture, and new aquaculture and mariculture systems

new contraceptive technologies adapted to the needs of potential users

greatly increased efforts to master widespread tropical diseases and disease vectors.

There are high potential payoffs to expanded research efforts at
both the largest and smallest scale of human interaction with the
natural environment.

In order to deal more effectively with research undertakings
of global scope, stronger international cooperation is needed, as
are greater use of technological opportunities to monitor environmental changes on a worldwide scale and much closer links between assessment and management. International scientific
organizations such as the Consultative Group on International Agricultural Research (CGIAR), the Special Committee on Problems
of the Environment (SCOPE) under the International Council of
Scientific Unions (ICSU), and the Coordinating Committee on the
Ozone Layer (CCOL) should be strengthened and should play a
stronger part in shaping the research agenda on global resource
problems, obtaining consensus on priorities, and coordinating efforts.

Similarly, efforts should be increased to create common met-
rics, definitions, and classification systems to improve the international compatibility of data bases. For example, standard
geographical formats would allow intercalibration of data from
surveys, satellite monitoring, and other sources. Remote sensing
technologies have the potential to revolutionize environmental
data collection and monitoring and should be accessible to Third
World as well as advanced industrial countries. An international

joint venture, along the lines of Intelsat, might be the appropriate model for making this technology widely available.

To remedy the deficiency of research into production systems and technologies relevant to the world's poor, there are a number of steps the scientific community itself can take. The scientific community and professional associations in the industrial countries can greatly expand linkages and cooperative programs with counterpart institutions in the Third World. Scientific exchanges and efforts to build stronger scientific institutions in developing nations can be expanded. The scientific community can also educate funding sources on the importance of research into technologies relevant to the poor and can powerfully influence the agendas of universities and other research institutions.

IMPLICATIONS FOR INTERNATIONAL ORGANIZATIONS

An enormous amount of concerted action will be required during the coming decades to deal with economic, security, and environmental questions of international or global scope. The need for intergovernmental organizations, particularly the U.N. system, able to facilitate cooperative actions among nations from which all can benefit has never been greater. International organizations can also contribute strongly to the exchange of expertise, the process of scientific research, and the mobilization and allocation of funding for important purposes.

To do this, international agencies require technical, managerial, and diplomatic skills of the highest order; a clear sense of purpose; and the support of national governments. Objective, accurate, technically competent, and well-directed staff work is effective in promoting international agreements and in building the confidence of national constituents in their international organizations. At present, some international agencies are regarded as first-rate in these respects; others are not.

Much of the present erosion of confidence stems from a lack of success in carrying out overly ambitious programs virtually designed for failure. Realistic expectations should focus on a reasonable agenda of high-priority activities. In the resource and environmental fields, while there are many problems common to most countries in the world, there are some that are inherently transboundary, or even of global scope, in that actions taken in one country directly inflict damages on others. Examples include long-range atmospheric pollution and climate modification, impacts on international waters and fisheries, and loss of biological diversity. International agencies play a useful role in building awareness and transmitting information about environmental problems of local or national scope but of concern to many countries. They have an essential role, however, in promoting international agreement to deal with problems that are beyond the power or outside the national interest of individual nations. A good example is the Mediterranean Regional Seas Program, in which UNEP played a critical role in coordinating assessment and research and facilitated intergovernmental agreements by drafting proposals and conducting discussions. Such international agencies should give greater priority to facilitating cooperative action by governments on environmental and other problems that are inherently transnational in scope.

There is serious concern about the ability of the present U.N. system to respond to these extraordinary challenges. The United Nations was born in hope, but there is now a pervasive feeling of despair about its effectiveness. Only through a strong commitment to fundamental change and with strong support from its member nations can it provide effective leadership in meeting critical issues arising from global interdependence.

IMPLICATIONS FOR INDUSTRIAL COUNTRY GOVERNMENTS

The industrialized and developing countries alike need good management of global resources at home and abroad: peace and prosperity in the industrial countries ultimately depend on access to needed resources and freedom from the risks of environmental disasters. This is truly one earth, and when dealing with resources that are global in character, the countries of the earth will sink or swim together. This basic fact bears frequent repetition, since it has not yet been adequately appreciated by policymakers or by the public in industrial countries. Support for efforts to improve management of resources is both a moral obligation of the industrial countries and in their direct interest.

Needed international action does not simply happen. Since national governments remain the principal actors at the international level, some countries must give global leadership if constructive action is to occur. Although industrial countries cannot and should not act alone, they have special opportunities for leadership. They dominate the world economy, have privileged access to means for action, and benefit most from progress and prosperity. The industrial countries have a higher national income than others, particularly when economic resources beyond the fulfillment of basic needs are taken into consideration, and consequently they have both the opportunity and the responsibility to assume a larger share of the load of paying for better management of global resources. Industrial countries also consume a disproportionate share of the world's resources. In fact, increased consumption of resources by industrial countries poses threats to global resources just as great as worldwide population increases, and measures to avert these threats can be taken by industrial countries themselves. Since they utilize a very large proportion of global resources either directly or indirectly, industrial countries' efforts to use them more efficiently will have a significant worldwide effect.

Resource management requires advanced scientific and technological capabilities and training facilities. The industrial countries predominate in these areas and experience many resource pressures and environmental problems before others. They therefore have valuable experience in their management. At the very least, there are lessons to be learned from industrial countries' past mistakes. Their privileged position in the global communications network must be used if these lessons of resource management are to be disseminated globally.

It is particularly important to show the economic significance of resource policy changes to establish the priority that is claimed for them in terms that can be understood by persons not directly involved in their development. Ultimately, action by democratic countries in favor of improved global resource and environmental management can only be expected if there is a strong public consensus that supports it, much as domestic environmental protection measures were supported by the public in industrial countries in the 1970s. Consequently, efforts to foster such support are important. To quote once again the participants in the Global Possible Conference, "We must mobilize now to achieve the global possible. If we do, the future can be bright. We have sufficient knowledge, skill, and resources—if we use them. If we remain inactive, whether through pessimism or complacency, we shall only make certain the darkness that many fear."

Index